TEACH YOURSELF BOOKS

Typing

Typing

Revised by Bettina Croft BA(Hons)Dip RSA

TEACH YOURSELF BOOKS

British Library Cataloguing in Publication Data

Library of Congress Catalog Card Number: 93-84982

First published in UK 1984 by Hodder Headline Plc, 338 Euston Road, London NW1 3BH

First published in US 1994 by NTC Publishing Group, 4255 West Touhy Avenue, Lincolnwood (Chicago), Illinois 60646 – 1975 U.S.A.

Copyright © 1984 Pitman Publishing

Printed in Great Britain by Cox & Wyman Ltd, Reading, Berkshire.

Impression number	12	11	10	9	8	7	6	5	4	3	
Year		1999	1998		1997		1996		1995		1994

——— CONTENTS ———

—— PREFACE ——

Most people want to be able to type quickly and accurately, prepare their own correspondence, understand handwritten manuscript work and display a variety of business documents. If you study this book you will rapidly be able to attain these goals with ease. Within this new edition emphasis throughout is on modern, more simple forms of newly accepted styles now found in offices, and all techniques are brought up to date.

This book has been specially designed for those who find it difficult to attend recognised training centres for regular personal tuition. The aim of attaining a good average speed of 40–50 words per minute has been allowed for by providing a section with speed tests which are simple to use and from which it is easy to work out your rate of progress. It is recommended that daily practice sessions are the ideal way of learning but, whatever time you can spend, the personal effort you put into practising is of vital importance.

This latest edition of *Teach Yourself Typing* has been carefully updated and revised extensively so that you can quickly master keyboard operation on any type of machine which uses the normal keyboards now found on today's latest typewriters, computers and word processors. Complete guidance is given on the most interesting and thorough ways of learning to operate these keyboards, and to develop accuracy at speed. The content has been devised using the most recent information available regarding developments in the computerised electronic office of today.

With this book you can quickly learn how to produce mailable letters, various types of frequently-used business documents, all your own personal correspondence, tabulated work and examples of other data now required in modern offices.

Linked themes have been introduced in this book and serve two purposes. Firstly, they give experience of personal real-life situations such as application forms for jobs, letters asking for bank loans and other documents on many topical subjects. Secondly, they are specifically designed to enable you to produce and keep a file of examples of personal correspondence which would be useful to refer to when dealing with real-life situations. This file of your best work could also form part of your own curriculum vitae to present as evidence of achievement when approaching a future employer for work.

—— INTRODUCTION ——

Since the days of the early typewriters there have been remarkable developments and improvements in their manufacture and many different models are now available. These include electric, electronic and portable typewriters weighing very little, and portable word processors/computers that can be used on aeroplanes and trains.

Electric and electronic models are now very popular because they produce a particularly clear typescript and have a wide range of facilities such as self-correcting devices, different symbols for specialist work and the facility to change the pitch. Some more sophisticated models provide a number of facilities similar to those available on word processors, including an emboldening capability for highlighting headings and a memory which allows the typewriter to 'remember' what has previously been typed – ranging from the last few characters or lines to whole paragraphs or pages, depending on the machine. The typist has the opportunity to use different typefaces within one document, use proportional spacing instead of normal, provide a justified right-hand margin, and to produce work which gives the appearance of printed pages. These developments have contributed to the efficient conduct of administrative work connected with business enterprises and the professions and, at the same time, have relieved the workload of the typist.

There has also been great progress in typewriting instruction, due not only to the provision of better equipment and excellent textbooks prepared specially for students and teachers, but also to the general acceptance of the importance of keyboard knowledge in the rapid expansion of information processing. It is also recognised that many more people should be acquainted with the standard 'Qwerty Keyboard' which is used in computer programming, compositing, electronic type-writing and the visual display unit in offices, airlines, and in many other applications. In this age of modern technology the word *keyboarding* takes on a new meaning.

Whilst recognising, however, that more and more sophisticated machines are coming on to the market, the essential elements of the typewriter remain unchanged. This book concentrates on the operation of manual and electric machines – ie those most likely to be used by beginners – whilst at the same time laying a foundation for the learner which remains embedded within modern technology.

1
TOUCH TYPING

The touch method

Today it is necessary first to learn touch typing in order to be a fast, accurate keyboard operator and to use the keyboard-controlled machines found in all modern offices.

This method has played an important part in typewriting progress since it is based on scientific principles. Typing by touch means that it is not necessary to glance from copy down to keyboard and back to what has been typed. The proficient typist locates the correct keys by touch and not by sight, and that is why blind people can become such excellent typists. Once learnt the movement becomes an automatic (subconscious) operation.

Each finger operates by relating only to the keys specifically allotted to it. Any confusion and strain are avoided as the fingers become, with practice, properly trained to respond instantly to the correct mental impulses and a reflex action occurs similar to the automatic effect of changing gears when driving a car. Eventually each finger moves in correct order to produce effortlessly a perfectly typed word.

The standard keyboard

The standard method of fingering is used throughout this book. It is a logical fingering system and is easily learnt. The layout of the keys is known as the 'Qwerty Keyboard' because of the word created by the first six letters of the row above the guide key row. The alphabet letters are divided into three rows in the following order:

In addition to these alphabet keys there are other keys for figures, fractions, commercial and other signs, and punctuation marks. Some of these do vary in position from one model to another.

As illustrated, the keyboard is divided into two approximately equal sections – one for each hand, and each finger is allotted a series of keys. The right thumb is used for the space bar.

Keyboard diagrams

A diagram of the complete keyboard is essential for self-tuition, as it will help in memorising the keys during the early stages of learning. In each of the following practice exercises and on the facing page there is a diagram showing the division of the typewriter keyboard, with a clear indication of the sections allotted to the fingers of each hand. It is necessary to refer to this frequently during the keyboard learning period in order to memorise the location of the keys.

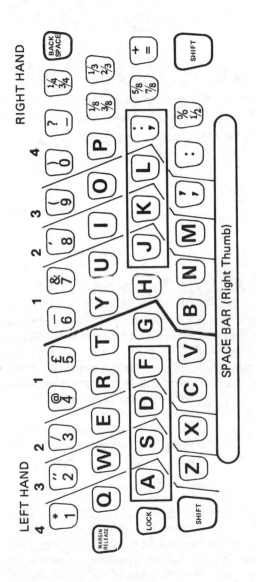

Division of the typewriter keyboard

2

THE PARTS AND —— CARE OF THE —— TYPEWRITER

—— **Parts of the typewriter** ——

Before keyboard instruction can begin, it is desirable to become acquainted with the most important parts of the typewriter. The details that follow relate to the parts of the manual machine brought into use during the keyboard learning stage and are illustrated opposite. Parts may vary between different manufacturers and the relevant manufacturer's handbook should always be consulted for operating instructions relating to either manual, electric or electronic machines.

The information that follows relates to the functions of various parts and to the general care of typewriters. It is given in alphabetical order to help any subsequent reference to a particular paragraph.

Back spacer (1)

This is usually situated at the top of the keyboard, at the extreme right or extreme left with an arrow pointing to the left, or containing the word 'Back-space'. This enables the operator to move the carriage backwards one space at a time. On an electric typewriter, however, the key will repeat its action until pressure is removed. When it is desired to move the carriage back a number of spaces, it is preferable to use the carriage release lever (3).

Bell, warning (1a)

The bell rings about six spaces before the point at which the right-hand margin stop has been set on manual machines.

The parts of the typewriter

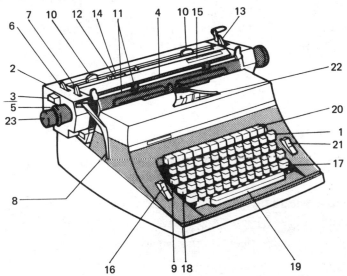

1 Back spacer	12 Paper gauge
2 Carriage	13 Paper release lever
3 Carriage release lever	14 Paper scale
4 Cylinder (or platen)	15 Paper table
5 Cylinder knobs	16 Ribbon switch
6 Interliner	17 Shift keys
7 Line space gauge	18 Shift lock
8 Line space and carriage	19 Space bar
return lever	20 Tabulator bar or key
9 Margin release	21 Touch control adjuster
10 Margin stops	22 Type basket
11 Paper bail and paper grips	23 Variable line spacer

Carriage (2)

The whole of the mechanism that travels across the top of the machine. On each depression of a key or the space bar, it moves one space from right to left. The carriage frame contains the cylinder (or platen), paper feed rollers, the line space mechanism, and margin and tabulator stops. In many modern machines, however, the type-head (golf ball or daisy wheel) moves while the carriage itself remains stationary.

Carriage release lever (3)

This lever may be situated at either or both ends of the carriage and, when depressed, enables the carriage to be moved independently of the escapement either to the right or to the left. It is used mainly when it is necessary to move the carriage a number of spaces beyond the point at which it is already standing – for example, to fill in details on a form or to make a correction.

Cylinder (4)

The cylinder (or platen) is the rubberised roller in the middle of the carriage, and it carries the paper in position.

Cylinder knobs (5)

Twirlers or hand-wheels fitted at each end of the cylinders; they are turned to move the paper into the required position for typing.

Interliner (6)

A lever situated to the left or right of the cylinder which, when moved forwards, frees the cylinder without the line of typing being lost. It is used when typing 'superior' characters or when it is necessary to type on ruled lines.

Line space gauge (indicator) (7)

This gauge is marked '1', '2', and '3', corresponding to three different line spaces, and the distance that the line space lever rotates the cylinder is determined by the setting of the gauge. There are six single-line spaces to the inch. On most modern typewriters, the line space gauge is marked for half-line spaces as well.

Line space (and carriage return) lever (manual) (8)

Used for turning up the paper when desired. At one operation the carriage is returned to the position set and the paper is ready for the beginning of a new line. This lever is struck with the left hand flat (palm downwards), so that the first finger carrying out the operation has the support of the other fingers.

On an electric typewriter the carriage is returned by striking a *key* on the right-hand side. It has a large arrow pointing to the left and is usually a much larger key than the back space. It is operated with the little finger of the right hand.

Margins (9)

It is useful to observe at this point that electronic machines and word processors have a different system for setting margins and it is necessary to programme their computers in order to set the required specific margins. With the 'word wrap' facility provided on modern equipment there is no need to return the carriage at the end of each line as the computer does this automatically for you unless instructed otherwise. Computerised margins are adjusted to the text that is keyed in to give either a ragged (uneven) or justified (straight) right-hand margin. It is therefore only necessary to press the electronic **return** key when there is an actual need for the line to end at a specific point. Normally, the electronic machine rolls on to the following line leaving the margin at the point set. (There is therefore no need for a warning bell to be sounded.)

Margin release (9a)

Depression of this key temporarily removes the set margin and permits the extension of the line of writing into the margin. The key may be indicated with an arrow pointing in two directions (left and right) or with the letters MR. Electric and electronic typewriters have different systems for releasing the margin and it is necessary to refer to the manual provided with the machine.

Margin stops (10)

Margins are regulated by the setting of the right-hand and left-hand margin stops at any desired position. These stops prevent movement of the carriage beyond a set point.

'On'/'Off' switch

This is the switch that controls the flow of current to an electric typewriter. It is important to check that the switch is in the 'off' position when the machine is not in use.

Paper bail (11)

The movable bar, which extends the width of the cylinder, on which the typing scale and paper grips are mounted. It holds the paper firmly against the cylinder when the keys are being struck.

Paper grips (11)

Adjustable paper clips or small rollers for holding the paper firmly in position.

Paper gauge (12)

This is an adjustable gauge that ensures that the left-hand edge of the paper is always inserted into the machine at the same point.

Paper release lever (13)

On depression of this lever the paper is free for proper adjustment or for removal from the machine.

Paper scale (14)

A gauge, marked or graduated, to coincide with the letter spaces; it indicates the length of the line of writing. There are twelve letter spaces to the inch in Elite type and ten in Pica type.

Paper table (15)

The paper rests on this metal plate behind the cylinder while it is being fed through the rollers.

Ribbons (16)

Electric and electronic machines use special cartridge ribbons as do the printers on word processors. Follow the manufacturer's instructions for replacing ribbons on all types of machines. Store all ribbons away from direct heat and sunlight.

Ribbon switch (16a)

There are three positions for this: (i) for using the top half of the ribbon, (ii) for using the lower half of the ribbon, and (iii) for disengaging the ribbon when a stencil is being cut.

Shift keys (17)

One on each side of the keyboard. They alter the position of the mechanism so that the capitals or upper-case and miscellaneous characters can be typed.

Shift lock (18)

This temporarily locks the typewriter so that continuous printing of capitals or upper-case and miscellaneous characters can take place. The shift lock can be released when the normal shift keys are pressed.

Space bar (19)

The long bar at the bottom of the keyboard is used to produce a space between words. Each time it is struck the carriage moves one space to the right. Always use the right thumb to operate the space bar. Electric typewriters and word processors have the facility of a repeating space bar which is achieved by holding down the bar which causes the spacing to be continuous until the thumb is lifted.

Tabulator bar or key (20)

On full depression of this bar or key the carriage moves rapidly to points previously set for the preparation of tabular work. The tabulator bar is set above the top row of keys, while the tabulator key is usually situated on the right-hand side of the keyboard.

Touch control adjuster (21)

A numbered selector switch that may either increase or decrease the tension on the typebars and thus enable the typist to adjust the machine to his or her own touch. If the operator experiences 'jumping' between characters in words, increase of tension will probably be the solution.

Type basket (22)

The name given to the segment that holds all the typebars. It is especially necessary to keep this part of the typewriter clear of eraser dust since otherwise the keys will not function properly.

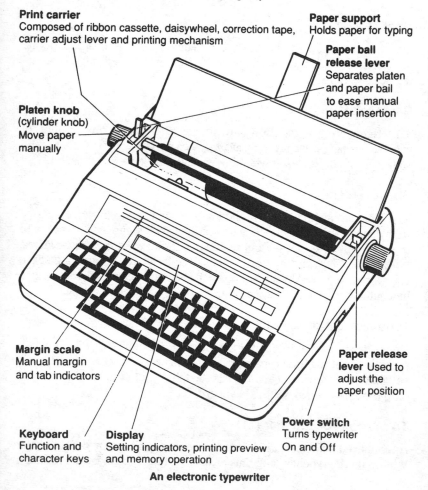

Print carrier
Composed of ribbon cassette, daisywheel, correction tape, carrier adjust lever and printing mechanism

Platen knob
(cylinder knob)
Move paper manually

Paper support
Holds paper for typing

Paper ball release lever
Separates platen and paper bail to ease manual paper insertion

Margin scale
Manual margin and tab indicators

Paper release lever Used to adjust the paper position

Keyboard
Function and character keys

Display
Setting indicators, printing preview and memory operation

Power switch
Turns typewriter On and Off

An electronic typewriter

Variable line spacer (23)

A knob at the end of the cylinder which frees the line space ratchet and allows for any desired spacing between lines of typewritten matter.

—————— Care of the typewriter ——————

Most of the text that follows applies to manual machines only. It is important to note that electric and electronic machines require regular maintenance by qualified experts. These machines are more fragile than manuals and are more sensitive to mishandling. It is also essential to follow the instructions on maintenance given in the handbook accompanying the machine. This should provide sensible advice about maintenance and care in use. If a handbook is not available it is worthwhile to contact the manufacturer who will be able to send you a copy. (*Warning* – Failure to follow the manufacturer's guidelines may result in loss of guarantee.)

Moving the machine

All types of electric, electronic and manual machines may have to be moved on occasions. Damage is often due to lack of care when moving the machine from one desk or table to another. Where possible, the carriage should be locked in a central position (either by the locking device on a portable typewriter or by moving the left- and right-hand margins towards the centre of the carriage on a manual).

With knees bent to avoid straining while lifting, place one hand under each side of the typewriter frame so that the full weight is taken. The typewriter should be carried with its key facing away from the body so that there is less danger of the keys becoming damaged or bent. Never lift the machine by holding each end of the cylinder. Hold the machine close to the body so that there is minimal strain on the back. *Always disconnect leads with electric and electronic machines and fold carefully around the machine* to avoid the possibility of anyone tripping over the cable.

Disregarding any of this advice and instruction may result in serious damage either to the machine being carried, or to the

person carrying it. Under HASWA (the Health and Safety at Work Act currently in force) the employee also has a personal responsibility to avoid accidents wherever possible by exercising sufficient care.

Dust

Modern electric and electronic machines have a self-correcting facility built into the ribbon mechanism whereby an error can be blanked out and the correct letters immediately retyped over the top.

In the past people have used rubber to eradicate errors on the typed page and this has been the chief cause of damage to the interior moving typewriter parts. Any accumulation of this rubber dust should be removed daily. When using rubber erasers, it is essential to prevent dust from falling into the mechanism, so move the carriage as far as possible to the left or to the right according to the position of the mistake to be erased. A long-handled brush should be used for removing dust and the action to follow is to brush away from the machine gently. However, by far the best method of eradicating errors is to use eradicating liquid or paper which prevents this problem.

Oiling of manual machines

A very small quantity of oil can be applied to manual typewriters using a fine nozzle on equipment obtainable from special office equipment stores, and this must only be applied at the point where friction occurs. Wipe away any visible excess immediately. On no account should oil be used on the typebars or in the segment in which the typebars move, because dust will adhere to oil and cause the bars to 'stick'. Only use oil from a typewriter company or firm marketing typewriter accessories.

Cleaning type of manual machines

The type itself may become clogged when a new ribbon is in use and the letters most needing attention are the 'closed' ones such as i, e, a, d, b, g, p and q, with w and v also. An effective way to remove dirt is to apply a little typewriter cleaning fluid to the type. A fairly stiff brush (specially designed for the purpose) should always be used and the movement required is forwards and backwards, *not* across the type basket which contains the typebars. Care must be taken *not* to brush too hard and dislodge the individual keys. There are also various useful cleaners on the market which can be purchased from office stationers.

Duplication of copies

It is now the usual practice in modern offices for work requiring duplication to be carried out using photocopying equipment. Carbon copying has been largely replaced by the photocopying method because it is labour-saving and cost effective. However, should the system of stencil cutting still be used, care must be taken to ensure that the type on the machine is specially cleaned and that a manual machine is used since most electric machines do not cut a satisfactory stencil.

Repairs

The question of repairs is seldom dealt with in typewriting manuals. It is possible for an experienced typist to make very minor adjustments to manual machines but it is essential, should any defect develop with electric or electronic machines, always to obtain the services of a skilled mechanic.

3

PRELIMINARIES —— TO KEYBOARD —— MASTERY

The main parts of the machine have now been noted, but there are still some important matters to be considered before keyboard operation can begin.

—————— Position at machine ——————

To carry out any machine work in an efficient manner it is generally agreed that a comfortable position will ensure complete command during operation, and the typewriter is no exception.

Furniture most suited for typewriting cannot always be secured, but an attempt should be made to adjust the height of the table and chair so that it is possible to sit comfortably. Wooden blocks, footrests and cushions can be used for this purpose. The beginner should sit with the elbows near the sides of the body and the forearms parallel to the slope of the typewriter keyboard.

When the machine has been placed with the bottom edge of the frame approximately in line with the front of the table, the typist should adopt a natural and easy position before the machine, with the body inclined slightly forwards. It is advisable to have an adjustable chair, fitted with a

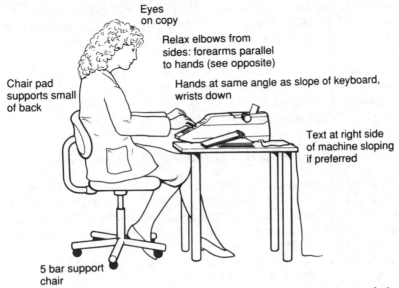

Eyes on copy

Relax elbows from sides: forearms parallel to hands (see opposite)

Chair pad supports small of back

Hands at same angle as slope of keyboard, wrists down

Text at right side of machine sloping if preferred

5 bar support chair

backrest but without arms, otherwise the proper movement of the forearms will be impeded.

During the depression of the keys, the backs of the hands should be kept perfectly level with the slope of the keyboard and the fingers should be bent at the middle joint. There should be very little movement of the wrist.

The feet should rest firmly on the floor, one slightly in front of the other in order to give balance to the body.

It is important that the typewriting table should be in a good light. The copy should be placed on the right-hand side of the machine so that the vision is not obstructed when the carriage return lever is operated, and care should be taken to ensure that shadows do not fall on the copy.

—— Paper insertion and removal ——

The method of inserting the paper is a simple operation and can be performed rapidly. Hold the paper to be inserted with the left hand and place it behind the cylinder so that it rests lightly on the feed rolls – the small rollers between the paper table and the cylinder. Ensure that the left-hand edge of the paper is against the paper gauge at '0'. Then 'switch' the paper into position with a quick turn of the right-hand cylinder knob. If the paper has not fed in evenly, it can be adjusted by using the paper release lever.

Withdrawal of the paper should also be done rapidly. The paper should be held at the top left-hand corner between the thumb and first finger of the left hand and lightly pulled at the same time as the paper release lever is operated. The paper can thus be removed quickly from the machine.

The backing sheet (manual machines only)

An improvement in the appearance of the typewritten work will be secured by the use of a backing sheet – a sheet of stout paper placed behind the typewriting paper – particularly when only one sheet of paper is required in the machine. A backing sheet helps to preserve the even surface of the cylinder, and a mark on the backing sheet will indicate when the bottom of the paper is being approached. A backing sheet ruled to show the side margins can also be helpful.

—— Depression of keys ——

Cultivate a light touch. Do not push or press the keys; tap them with a light, quick blow, and this will ensure a clear and sharp impression. After a little practice the operator will be able to judge the degree of pressure that is necessary to obtain the best result. The finger must leave the key immediately on depression, so that the typebar is not restricted in its downward movement. Punctuation marks require a lighter touch than that used for the other keys. A heavy depression of the full stop, comma and hyphen is likely to puncture the paper on manual machines.

The operator of an electric typewriter requires considerably less force than a manual machine and the hands tend to be held flatter because the keyboard is less steep. Pressure is regulated by the machine.

Rhythm

The beginner will find it helpful when learning new key reaches to type each letter to a conscious rhythm. However, as the typing skill develops, it will be found that rhythm has less to do with the typing of each letter and more to do with the patterns contained within words and word groups.

Type sizes

The sizes of typewriter type in most general use are Elite and Pica. There are twelve letters to the inch for Elite type. Pica type is a larger type, and there are ten letters to the inch. The exercises in the keyboard mastery sections are shown in Pica type. It will require a very elementary arithmetical calculation to ascertain the space required for a line containing a similar number of letters of Pica and Elite. A line of writing containing sixty characters (or a space in lieu of a character) of Pica type will occupy six inches, but the same number of characters in Elite type will take up only five inches.

Paper

International Paper Sizes A4 (8¼ in × 11¾ in; 210 mm × 297 mm) and A5 (5⅞ in × 8¼ in; 148 mm × 210 mm) are in common use in Britain. Good-quality paper is always more economical since both sides can be used.

The following table gives the number of spaces across a page of A4 and A5 in both Elite and Pica, and the number of lines to the page.

	A4	A5 (shorter side at top)	A5 (longer side at top)
Spaces across the page			
Elite (12 to 2.5 cm or 1 in)	100	70	100
Pica (10 to 2.5 cm or 1 in)	82	59	82
Lines down the page			
Elite and Pica (both 6 lines to the inch)	70	50	35

Different styles in typewritten material

That typewriting should be done by 'touch' is beyond dispute, but apart from definite methods of operation, there are few hard-and-fast rules regarding the production of an ordinary piece of typescript. However, the blocked method of layout, whereby all the lines of letters and other documents begin at the left-hand margin, is in wide use. This method saves time and has a clear, pleasing appearance. Open punctuation, which is usually used in conjunction with blocked layout, saves further time and will also be discussed later in the book (page 79).

The more traditional styles, involving indented paragraphs (usually 1/2 inch – 5–6 spaces – from the left-hand margin), centred headings, etc., are still preferred by some, and individual organisations will often specify the style to be used.

Whatever the method, consistency is important.

4

KEYBOARD MASTERY: THE GUIDE KEY ROW

(SECOND ROW)

The most important section of the typewriter keyboard will naturally receive first consideration. It consists of eight keys in the second row from the space bar, known as the 'home keys', and from these keys the sense of location of all the other keys will be developed.

These home keys are **a s d f** for the fingers of the left hand and **; l k j** for the fingers of the right hand. They are often referred to as the 'guide keys', although it is generally considered that the guide keys are the two home keys operated by the little fingers – **a** and **;**. The following diagram shows the arrangement of the home keys (the boxed-in sections):

During keyboard operation the tips of the fingers indicated in the diagram should rest lightly (so lightly that there is no actual depression of the keys) on the home keys. The little finger of the left hand operates **a**, and the third, second and first fingers the remaining keys for the left section – **s d f**. The little finger of the right hand operates the semicolon

(;), and the third, second and first fingers the remaining keys for the right section – **l k j**.

Repeat aloud several times **a s d f** and **; l k j**, in this order, and during the repetition tap the respective fingers on the table at equal intervals of time – one tap a second – as mentioned under 'Rhythm' on page 16. This will give a clear picture of what is required.

Then feed a sheet of paper (with backing sheet) into the machine for the first exercise; set the margin stops at 25 and 75 (Elite type) or 16 and 66 (Pica type), and return the carriage to the left-hand margin stop for the beginning of the first line. Set the line space gauge for single-line spacing.

Place your fingers on the home keys, as shown on the diagram on page 19. Every time you remove your left hand from the keyboard to return the carriage at the end of a line, or operate the carriage-return key on an electric typewriter, you must be able to return your fingers to their home keys *without looking at the keyboard*.

Each key should be struck lightly and at equal intervals of time – one stroke a second until repeated practice makes an increase to two strokes a second possible. It is essential at this stage that there should be absolute accuracy and even depression of the keys; speed will come with regular practice.

Place the copy on the right-hand side of the typewriter. This will prevent the copy from being hidden by the left forearm when the carriage is returned. Make sure that it is in such a position that you can read the exercises easily without having to alter your position at the machine.

The four keys memorised for the left hand (**a s d f**) are required for the first line of Exercise 1 (on page 22), and, with the eyes on the copy, this combination of letters is to be repeated twelve times. While the home keys for the left hand are being struck for the first line, the fingers of the right hand should be resting lightly on their respective keys. The line numbers are inserted for reference only, and the reminders given with the exercises should be carefully noted before starting to type.

When the end of each line is reached, the carriage on manual machines should be returned to the right of the machine by contacting the carriage return level with the side of the first finger of the left hand (palm downwards); this finger should be supported by the other fingers of this hand. If this lever is struck smartly, the double action of turning up the paper for the next line and returning the carriage to the left-hand margin stop will be accomplished.

During the return of the carriage, the right hand keeps its home key position and the left returns to the home keys immediately on completion of the carriage return movement.

Now note the second line. This deals with the four keys memorised for the right hand (**; l k j**) and completes the eight home keys. The fingers of the left hand should be in the normal home keys position during the typing of the second line.

In the third and fourth lines the additional keys (**g** and **h**) are introduced; they are shown in the diagram at the head of the exercises. The first finger of the left hand will move slightly to the right from **f** to **g**, and the first finger of the right hand will move slightly to the left from **j** to **h**. The other fingers should not be moved when the additional key is struck. Immediately after the depression of **g** or **h** the finger should return to its home key. Each series of letters in these lines finishes on the home keys for the first fingers – **f** and **j**.

For the fifth and sixth lines the order has been varied. Repeated practice will ensure that, as each letter is read, the appropriate finger will respond to the direction by the brain and depress the key for the letter shown in the copy.

A space is required after each series of letters in the fifth and sixth lines, and the space bar should always be struck with the right-hand thumb, but the fingers should not leave their home key positions. The time taken for the depression of the space bar should be equal to that for a letter or character key; in this way correct rhythm will be maintained.

Each line in the exercises should be treated as a separate item and copied three times. For repetition practice, type in single-line spacing. After the repeated practice on each line, type in double-line spacing at least one accurate copy of the whole exercise.

More work with the space bar is given in Exercise 2, and Exercises 3 and 4 consist of words built up from the home keys and the additional keys for the first finger of each hand.

After finishing each exercise examine the work and circle any mistakes in pencil. Find out the cause of any errors – uneven key depression, wrong fingers, etc – and then type the corrections several times. If any of the typed letters are 'shadowed', it can be assumed that the keys are being pressed, instead of being tapped with a staccato movement.

Apart from the question of accuracy, work produced on a manual machine should be examined from the point of view of evenness of touch. There should not be varying shades of thickness; each letter should have the appearance of having had the same intensity of depression. If some

Exercise 1

1. asdfasdfasdfasdfasdfasdfasdfasdfasdf

2. ;lkj;lkj;lkj;lkj;lkj;lkj;lkj;lkj;lkj

3. asdfgfasdfgfasdfgfasdfgfasdfgfasdfgf

4. ;lkjhj;lkjhj;lkjhj;lkjhj;lkjhj;lkjhj

5. fdsa jkl; fdsa jkl; fdsa dfas kj;l dfas

6. sfad lj;k sfad lj;k sfad sadf l;kj sadf

7. dad; sad; lad; lass; falls; fads; gag; flag; has;

8. a lass falls; dad has flags; a sad lad has a fad;

9. glass; gala; saga; flask; salad; jag; lash; gash;

10. a lad had a gag; a glass flask; dad adds a salad;

Exercise 2

1. as ad af ag ;l ;k ;j ;h as ad af ag ;l ;k ;j ;h

2. ;l ;k ;j ;h as ad af ag ;l ;k ;j ;h as ad af ag

3. as ;l ad ;k af ;j ag ;h as ;l ad ;k af ;j ag ;h

4. sa l; da k; fa j; ga h; sa l; da k; fa j; ga h;

5. sd df sd df lk kj lk kj sd df sd df lk kj lk kj

6. gf fg gf fg jh hj jh hj gf fg gf fg jh hj jh hj

7. hall; halls; flash; shall; hag; gas; sags; daffs;

8. gala flags; a sad saga; a glass hall; daffs fall;

9. sash; dash; slash; hash; ask; galas; sagas; gags;

10. jags dash; sad sagas; dad asks a gag; glass sash;

Reminders: set margin stops at 25 and 75 (Elite type) or 16 and 66 (Pica type); adopt correct position at keyboard; do not look at keyboard; fingers to rest lightly on home keys; right-hand thumb for space bar depression; equal intervals between each key depression; one stroke a second; the line numbers are for reference only. Type each line three times.

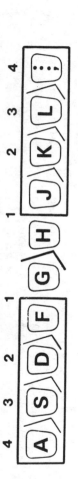

Exercise 3

1. sad; lag; sad; lag; sad; lag; sad; lag;
2. jag; has; jag; has; jag; has; jag; has;
3. fad; ask; fad; ask; fad; ask; fad; ask;
4. lad; aha; lad; aha; lad; aha; lad; aha;
5. gas; ash; gas; ash; gas; ash; gas; ash;
6. had; sag; had; sag; had; sag; had; sag;
7. dad has had a flag; ask a gag; has a flask glass;
8. flask; flasks; gala; galas; fad; fads; gas; lash;
9. add a gag; lads had fads; ash falls; glass flask;
10. gala salads; all flags fall; a lass adds a glass;

Exercise 4

1. dash; half; dash; half; dash; half;
2. lass; glad; lass; glad; lass; glad;
3. gall; shag; gall; shag; gall; shag;
4. flask shall flask shall flask shall
5. salad glass salad glass salad glass
6. galas flags galas flags galas flags
7. half a flag; glass hall; glad gag; flasks fall;
8. hags; sall; lags; dall; fall; slag; sags; lass;
9. dads ask; gas adds; a lass falls; half a salad;
10. all had salad; shall a lad dash; dad has a jag;

Reminders: right-hand thumb for space bar depression; first finger returns at home key after striking additional key; little movement of the wrists. Type each line three times.

fingers appear to be weak (and very often this is the case with the little fingers), there should be additional practice with the letters that show any such weakness.

Finally, remember that this first stage of keyboard mastery is of special importance; it is with this second row of keys that the remainder of the keyboard is associated, and extended practice on the exercises will be well worth the time spent in this way.

5

KEYBOARD MASTERY: ——— THE TOP ——— ALPHA ROW

(ROW ABOVE GUIDE KEYS)

The top row of the alpha keyboard includes ten additional letters of the alphabet, five for the fingers of each hand. The order in which they appear is shown in the following diagram:

As you have practised the guide keys in the previous chapters you should now find it possible to reach up from these keys to the row immediately above and this is the row from which the design of the keyboard gets its name – 'Qwerty'.

Each finger has to reach up to cover an additional key, **a** to **q**, **s** to **w**, **d** to **e**, and so on, with the exception of the forefinger of each hand which, being stronger, covers two keys on the row above. The left forefinger moves from **f** to **t** and **f** to **r**, and the right from **j** to **y** and **j** to **u**. *The remaining keys follow logically: k to i, l to o, ; to p. Remember to keep your fingers hovering over the guide keys and reach up to strike the correct key. Do not lift the whole hand up one row.*

The following exercises contain some fingering drills incorporated into the keyboard training which will enable you to 'feel' your way up the keyboard to locate the required key, for example:

```
aqa sws ded frf
juj kik lol ;p;
ftf jyj ftf jyj
```

These are swiftly followed by words containing the new row of letters so that meaningful practice can take place using your new ability to type the extra vowels, **i** and **e**.

Practise:

```
see lee fees deed
die lies fie kids
```

You will see that the forefingers of each hand have four times as much work to do since not only do they also cover **g** and **h** on the guide key row, but are used to reach up and across for **r** and **u**, and finally across and upwards for **t** and **y**.

Practise:

```
fit feet fate jay hat hit yes yet
```

Your fingers will now be working in harmony to cover the whole of these two rows of the keyboard. You will also rapidly progress to the shift keys so that individual words with capital letters can be typed.

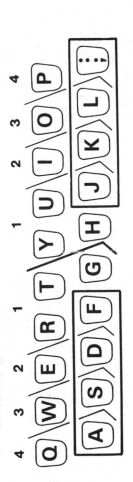

Exercise 5

1. aqa ;p; aqa ;p; aqa ;p; aqa ;p; aqa ;p;
2. sws lol sws lol sws lol sws lol sws lol
3. ded kik ded kik ded kik ded kik ded kik
4. frf juj frf juj frf juj frf juj frf juj
5. ftf jyj ftf jyj ftf jyj ftf jyj ftf jyj
6. gtg hyh gtg hyh gtg hyh gtg hyh gtg hyh
7. see sea lee lea tee tea the she fee gee gea
8. jeer fear leaf hear gear dear deer here peer rear
9. he fears the sea; she sees a dear rear; tea leaf;
10. she sees the red dear is here; they all hear her;

Exercise 6

1. aqw ;po aqw ;po aqw ;po aqw ;po aqw ;po
2. swe loi swe loi swe loi swe loi swe loi
3. der kiu der kiu der kiu der kiu der kiu
4. frt juy frt juy frt juy frt juy frt juy
5. gtr hyu gtr hyu gtr hyu gtr hyu gtr hyu
6. qaw p;o wse oli edr iku qaw p;o wse oli edr iku
7. are is that was its at to this were few get you
8. pot spot quote equity query pro pride pear poorer;
9. it was quoted; there were a few; he spots a query;
10. was that a spot; that was poor; his pride appears;

Reminders: find home keys position without looking at the keyboard; the touch should be as light as possible; time for depression of space bar the same as for character key; examine work, encircle all errors and type corrections several times.

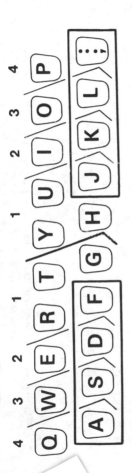

Exercise 7

1. lap fit hay pay dog key for hye fur jay foes figs
2. deaf poll free pill gear oily tear holy read hill
3. hoop star hull lead loop dare steep gate pull fry
4. she feared steep hills; they pulled the dogs free
5. flay dial work goal fury girl dual dish fowl quay
6. spelt prowls shapes lapel shale palsy queue furls
7. ladder dapper figure shallow ferret dagger gossip
8. keep deaf ears to all gossip; the sea was shallow
9. fit the seat tightly; pull the dagger out please;
10. two star ships are early; today there are queues;

Exercise 8

Consolidation

*All these sentences are based on letters and/or words already practised in Exercises
1–7 inclusive.*

1. they are sure that they were right at that period

2. at their request the first few words were deleted

3. there is a good supply of hot water at this hotel

4. goods like those are sure to get you the top rate

5. he helped us to pass the press proofs of the list

6. the guard said that the lads had paid their fares

7. what was it that he saw at their park gates today

8. are there ladders outside the new houses for sale

9. he feared to tell her that they saw a yellow star

10. the queues were to the right of the theatre doors

*Reminders: the hand not typing should remain in home keys position; examine work
for accuracy and evenness of touch.*

6

KEYBOARD MASTERY:
— THE BOTTOM ROW —
(ROW BELOW GUIDE KEYS)

Having successfully mastered the guide key row and the row above, you can now progress to the remaining alphabetic keys on the bottom row. Study this diagram carefully.

The movement of your fingers downwards and slightly to the left is necessary for the bottom row of keys. The reason that there is nothing, as yet, for the fourth finger (or little finger) on the left hand to do is that it is reserved for stretching across to the individual shift key on that side (which is dealt with fully in Chapter 8). For the present all that is necessary is to reach down from the letter **a** to the larger key marked SHIFT on the extreme left-hand side of the bottom row which, when depressed, apparently does nothing. It does not move the carriage but, when used in conjunction with an alpha key, forms an individual capital letter.

The following finger reaches require considerable perseverance in practising. Make sure that you first locate your fingers over the guide keys and then reach down to type with the third finger of the left hand:

szs szs szs szs szs szs szs

Do not allow the whole hand to move down the keyboard.

Using the third finger of the right hand reach down and type the comma.

l,l,l,l,l,l,l,l,l,l,l,l,l,l,l

Then using the fourth finger (little finger) of the right hand reach down from the semicolon to the full stop. (This finger will also cover the right-hand shift key in Chapter 8.)

;.;.;.;.;.;.;.;.;.;.;.;.;

Continue to practise the following reaches downwards first with the middle finger of the left hand and then with middle finger of the right until you can build up speed.

dxd dxd dxd dxd dxd dxd dxd

kmk kmk kmk kmk kmk kmk kmk

Finally, when you have practised all the fingering drills above to develop speed, progress to the reaches downwards from **f** to **c** with the left forefinger and then from **j** to **n** with the right forefinger:

fcf fcf fcf fcf jnj jnj jnj jnj

fcf fcf fcf fcf jnj jnj jnj jnj

You will notice again that the forefingers are doubling up on their workloads as they have also to cover the reaches across to **v** and **b** respectively (you will find stretching across to **b** needs practice):

fvf fvf fvf fvf fvf fvf fvf fvf

jbj jbj jbj jbj jbj jbj jbj jbj jbj

For the following exercises, keep hands hovering over the guide key rows and reach down to the keys. Practise each word for at least two lines before starting the sentences, and practise each fingering drill several times.

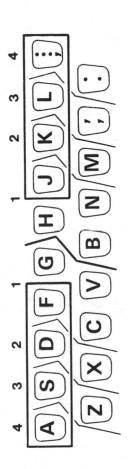

Exercise 9

1. szs l,l szs l,l ;.; ;.; ;.; ;.; ;.; ;.;
2. dxd kmk dxd kmk fcf jnj fcf jnj fcf jnj
3. fvf jbj fvf jbj fvf jbj fvf jbj fvf jbj
4. zxz ,m, cvc nbn zxz ,m, cvc nbn cvc nbn
5. zoo man ebb car oxo mop van mad axe box ace coz
6. many boxes of mops can go to the zoo in the car
7. cat but cut not cot vet bet men eve ivy cry nib
8. a quiet time means less work for the van driver
9. zones mends above caters vendors bending oxygen
10. see how delicate the ozone layer is above earth

Exercise 10

1. asz ;l, asz ;l, asz ;l, sdx lkm sdx lkm sdx lkm
2. dfc kjn dfc kjn dfc kjn fgv jhb fgv jhb fgv jhb
3. green fields and trees enable us to breathe air
4. aqa ;p. swz lo, dex kim frc jun gtv hyb aqa ;p.
5. p.p ,o, ex mim nib mid ice buzz nor inn own vie
6. ever nun viva bye buy ivy cot bat lobs mug tops
7. our batsmen played two very exciting games today.
8. time zone over lick oboe mean have care come zeal
9. cats have much more zeal in chasing mice than men
10. the new world time zones do vary by several hours

*Reminders: set your own margin stops; eyes on copy; note downward movement
from second row; full depression of shift key in the same time as that taken for
character key.*

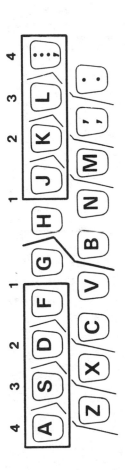

Exercise 11

1. cab ham van bad nag jam dab ban sax cad jab fan

2. and can mad lax bag jag bat nab ham act dam man

3. amend label flame naval panel glebe brake snake

4. visor brick clays urban vodka codes lapel horse

5. chair mango docks neigh widow shame broth slant

6. sings penal chant handy spent chaos bench cycle

7. the cab came and the van went; mend the dam now

8. money well spent; labels are handy; red flames;

9. horses neigh; penalty codes are amended yearly;

10. extra time must be spent on exercises and diet;

Exercise 12

1. face limb raze boil axe, the man can act and sing
2. cave bulk fact lion fax, ban jam and eat more veg
3. gave join care tame arc, can lions live in caves;
4. vast act ban wave exit, boil the bulk of the ham;
5. milk plum pun act over, the docks had vast waves;
6. hymn bin vase ice daze, urban areas have no cabs;
7. bulk oil is often used for new cars in the garage
8. save birthday cards for various charities to use.
9. plum and apple trees need careful pruning yearly.
10. the calcium contained in milk is very beneficial.

Reminders: cultivate a light and even touch; do not look at the keyboard – eyes on the copy; examine typewritten work, encircle errors and type correct words.

7
KEYBOARD MASTERY: THE FIGURE AND SYMBOL ROW
(ROW AT VERY TOP OF KEYBOARD)

You can now type 26 letters of the alphabet, and punctuation marks for the semicolon, comma and full stop.

This chapter includes the figure row of keys which introduces the arabic numbers (1 to 0), and the hyphen. It may be found on some machines that keys are not provided for arabic 1 and 0 but these figures can be obtained by typing the small letter '1' and the capital letter 'O' instead. *Never use a capital letter 'I' as this is used for roman numerals only.*

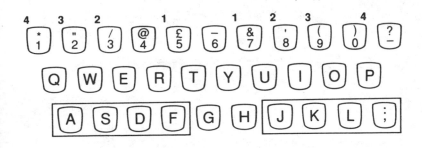

From the diagram (on page 39) you can see that other signs are also on the upper portion of each figure key. These are obtained by using the shift keys in conjunction with the figure key.

The forefingers of each hand will again double their workload as **4** and **5** have to be operated with left forefinger and **6** and **7** with the right forefinger. The reach from the guide key row is further than you have experienced so far and is slightly to the left of the corresponding keys in the top alpha row.

Again remember to keep the fingers hovering above the guide keys. Strike the relevant guide key, then the key from the row above and then reach up to the figure.

```
aq1  sw2  de3  fr4  gt5
hy6  ju7  ki8  lo9  ;p0
```

As you can see, the little finger of the right hand also reaches up and across to the right for the hyphen thus:

```
;p-  ;p-  p;-  p;-  ;p-  p;-
```

In the exercises that follow the above movements have been incorporated with practice provided to cover the whole keyboard, including numbers. Chapter 8 deals with the symbols in the figure and symbol row.

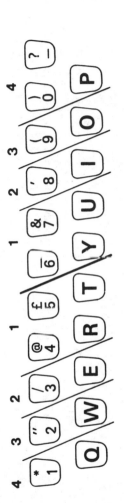

Exercise 13

1. aq1 ;p0 aq1 ;p0 aq1 ;p0 sw2 1o9 sw2 1o9 sw2 1o9

2. de3 ki8 de3 ki8 de3 ki8 fr4 ju7 fr4 ju7 fr4 ju7

3. gt5 hy6 gt5 hy6 gt5 hy6 aq1 ;p0 sw2 1o9 de3 ki8

4. you have 27 benches and 93 chairs in stock now;

5. it will be 17 May today, and tomorrow is 18 May

6. 720K computers can now store 7000 new addresses

7. margins of 28 and 86 are used for text no 36780

8. he came – he saw – and then he conquered us all

9. shopping list – tea, bacon, 12 eggs, 2 lb sugar

10. 423,891 people will now be coming from 56 areas

Exercise 14

You may find the dash in a different place on some machines.

1. a1a ;0; a1a ;0; a1a ;0; s2s 191 s2s 191 s2s 191

2. d3d k8k d3d k8k d3d k8k f4f j7j f4f j7j f4f j7j

3. g5g h6h g5g h6h g5g h6h 132 425 262 728 293 038

4. numbers – 145 8979, 041–678 59403, 051–270 9634

5. the conjurer used 149 boxes – 16 tricks in each

6. typewriters locate the dash on different keys –

7. please post leaflets to flats 39, 41, 45 and 63

8. he telephoned the new 661, 667, and 678 series.

Reminders: the letter 'l' may be used for the numeral 'one'; lighter depression of punctuation marks.

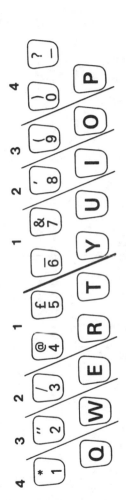

Exercise 15

Top row numbers are standard to most machines but there is a variation in the symbols which are obtained by using the shift key.

1. top 123 pip 345 try 678 our 132 pie 354 now 687

2. 213 rye 435 wet 768 toe 231 raw 453 pop 786 eye

3. pop try the top row – our 78 red cups were gone

4. put 3770 and 3120 out – the toy pup was too wet

5. all the 79 men cut the 40 yew trees and 56 oaks

6. quotes are very low for orders of 3,000 or more

Exercise 16

1. tree 1234 weep 3456 peer 5678 quip 7890 prop 4321
2. rope 2342 wept 4563 pert 6785 part 9780 tour 2341
3. write your name on the list for tour number 46593
4. now order 360 spare tyres for your 19 office cars
5. look at part 7 and type out the 8th on micro card
6. pier 59 needs rope from the bulk naval store room
7. & is called an ampersand, and @ is the 'at' sign.
8. / is named 'slash' and is used for references etc
9. ' is single quotation mark or used for apostrophe
10. an asterisk is *, and " is used for double quotes

Reminders: keep eyes on copy during keyboard operation; encircle all errors and type
corrections several times.

8

SHIFT KEYS
— AND COMBINATION —
CHARACTERS

—————— Shift keys and shift lock ——————

Each of the 46 character keys operate typebars on which are fitted two characters, and these may include a small (lower-case) and capital (upper-case) alphabetical character, a figure, a commercial sign, a punctuation mark or a fraction. The keyboard diagram on page 48 shows all the miscellaneous characters and signs on the top portion of the keys. However, you may find that the characters above numbers vary and some, like back spacer, %, ?, $ and ! are found in different locations on some keyboards. Do find out where they are on your own particular machine.

For the capital letters and miscellaneous characters the shift keys are necessary – they move the cylinder or the type segments for the correct type impression. There is a shift key on each side of the keyboard, usually at each end of the bottom row of keys. The shift keys are operated by the little fingers. If the character required is on the right-hand side of the keyboard, the left shift key must be depressed, and vice versa.

Careful practice is essential to secure correct depression of the shift key. It is different from that for the ordinary key depression, as the shift key is fully depressed and held down during the striking of the character key on the opposite side of the keyboard. The timing of this depression should be the same as for a character key – and ensure that there is no break in the rhythm. The finger should return to its normal home key position immediately the shift key is released.

The shift lock is depressed when several capital letters are to be typed in succession.

The first practice for shift key operation will deal with associated keys of the second, third and fourth rows. The capitals (use of shift keys) are given for the second row, the lower-case letters for the third row and the miscellaneous characters (use of shift keys) for the fourth row. On some machines, the keys may differ from those shown for the top row. The appropriate alterations should therefore be made.

Depress the right-hand shift key to its full extent and use the little finger of the left hand to type **A**; release the shift key and then type the lower-case letter in the third row for the same finger **q**, and again depress the right-hand shift key to type the asterisk (*****) in the top row. Repeat these movements several times, as:

Aq* Aq* Aq* Aq* Aq* Aq* Aq* Aq*

Now combine the remaining keys for the left hand in the three rows under construction, as:

```
Sw" Sw" Sw" Sw" Sw" Sw" Sw" Sw"
De/ De/ De/ De/ De/ De/ De/ De/
Fr@ Fr@ Fr@ Fr@ Fr@ Fr@ Fr@ Fr@
Gt£ Gt£ Gt£ Gt£ Gt£ Gt£ Gt£ Gt£
```

Similar movements by the right hand and the depression of the left-hand shift key will complete the remaining six upper-case characters of the top row. Type six lines, as:

```
:p) :p) :p) :p) :p) :p) :p) :p)
:p? :p? :p? :p? :p? :p? :p? :p?
Lo( Lo( Lo( Lo( Lo( Lo( Lo( Lo(
Ki' Ki' Ki' Ki' Ki' Ki' Ki' Ki'
Ju& Ju& Ju& Ju& Ju& Ju& Ju& Ju&
Hy_ Hy_ Hy_ Hy_ Hy_ Hy_ Hy_ Hy_
```

Upper-case characters are contained in the three outside character keys of the bottom (or first) row; they are on the typebars already operated for the comma, full stop and ½ fraction. The comma usually appears twice on one typebar, as does the full stop. Over the ½ fraction is usually the per cent sign.

Depress the left-hand shift key to its full extent, and with the third right finger strike the key for the bottom row (the comma); with the little finger strike the key to the right (the full stop), without shift key depression, and again depress the shift key while the little finger moves to the right to strike the key for the per cent sign, as:

, .% , .% , .% , .% , .% , .% , .% , .%

Ordinarily, it would not be necessary to release the shift key for the full stop, but the above combination is given for practice in the use of the shift key.

In the exercises which follow, do not forget to use the individual shift keys for symbols. In line one of Exercise 17 there is a shift key to type first, then an alpha key and then the symbol.

When underlining a word, use the backspace key to return to the beginning of the word, use shift lock plus the underscore key, and then release the lock.

All the alphabet letters, punctuation marks and miscellaneous characters are included in Exercise 19, which provides excellent practice covering the major part of the keyboard. The shift lock will be used when underscoring in the third line.

Exercise 20 is arranged for shift lock practice, and the lock will have to be released for the typing of the dash (or hyphen) between the items in the list of subjects.

The top row containing arabic numerals and miscellaneous characters is not easy to memorise, and the diagram given at the head of the exercises in this chapter includes this row and shows its association with the third row.

Roman numerals

When roman numerals are required, they are compiled from the following letters – capital or small:

```
I  (1);    V    (5);   X  (10);
L (50);    C  (100);   D (500);
           M (1000);
```

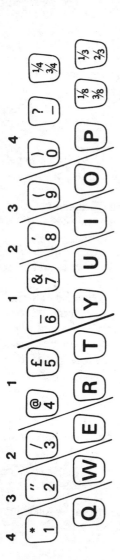

Exercise 17

1. Aq* :p) Sw" Lo(De/ Ki' Fr@ Ju& Gt£ Hy_ :p? ,%:
2. Anne Sue Don Fay Gil Hal Jim Kay Len May Ben Sam
3. Quite Pins Wit Our Eat Idea Rags Urge Tops Yours
4. Jay had a 90% pass in Maths, 95% in French Oral.
5. The Prime Minister met the President of the USA.
6. Our Pin Number was "secret" to the bank's files.
7. Janice Hayward & Sons, 34 & 35 Bond Street, Ely.
8. (Please use this letter reference – DER/HL/968).
9. David Lee caught 47 trout and paid £43 for them.
10. Did Mary and Natalie go to 28 Euro Disney shows?

Exercise 18

Alphabetic coverage of capital letters

1. Areas by the Lakeland Park are full of Red Deer.

2. New Zealand is a country for new Olympic Awards.

3. Uncle Fred found a Roman sword at Castle Coombe.

4. Quite a few Western Greek fashions arrive daily.

5. Xerox copies of Val's Intermediate Certificates.

6. Yes, Pearl Divers were saved from the Black Sea.

7. Runnymede is where King John signed Magna Carta.

8. Had Ted negotiated new contracts for Ed and Lee?

Reminders: little fingers to operate shift keys; shift key to be fully depressed and held during the striking of the character key.

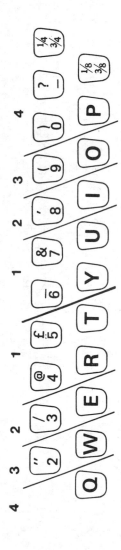

Exercise 19

1. Bizet & Co offered us this page (6" x 8") for £9.

2. Ted's quotations are: 18/20p or 30/35p per kilo.

3. Please send, by the end of this week, a cheque for £247.

4. Colon (:) and semicolon (;) appear on the one key.

5. Their invoice was for 5 copies @ 65p, less 12½%. *

6. Will John send them another copy of this 70p book?

Exercise 20

Remember to use the shift lock for this exercise, but this has to be released in order to obtain the dash between each item.

Apart from the famous Teach Yourself Typing book
the series includes the following:-

ASTROLOGY – BIOLOGY – CHEMISTRY – MARKETING – BADMINTON
PHYSICS – ELECTRICITY – INDONESIAN – CROQUET – GEOMETRY
ELECTRONICS – SOCIOLOGY – MATHEMATICS – MUSIC – ALGEBRA
TAXATION – PORTUGUESE – CALCULUS – JAPANESE – ECONOMICS
AUDIO-TYPING – PHOTOGRAPHY – SHORTHAND – WORDPROCESSING

Reminder: set margin stops for both exercises at 22 and 80 Elite type and at 12 and 70 Pica type.

Capitals are used for numbers with names of monarchs, chapter headings, acts in plays and books of the Bible, and for numbering paragraphs when it is not convenient to use arabic numerals:

`Elizabeth II   Chapter XX   Act I`

Paragraphs in business letters are usually numbered in lower case, for example:

`i), ii) and iii)`

Small letters are also commonly used for numbering the preliminary pages of a book, and for enumerating sub-paragraphs or subsections, scenes in plays or chapters in books:

`page vi   Scene iii   I Corinthians iv, 2`

When working out Roman numerals it is necessary to remember that a letter placed *before* one of greater value indicates that the first number is deducted from the second to find the total, for example, to obtain 40 take X (10) away from L (50) = XL.

A letter placed *after* one of greater value indicates the two are added:

> to obtain 60 add X (10) to L (50)   = LX
> to obtain 20 add X (10) to X   = XX
> to obtain 25 add XX to V (5)   = XXV

A line placed over any Roman symbol indicates that its value is multiplied by 1000. Roman numerals should be lined up underneath each other, either to the right or the left. (Further examples are on pages 156 and 223.)

_____ Combination characters and _____ special signs

Should your manual machine not be provided with any of the following useful combined characters (ie those made with one character superimposed over another) then you need to know how to produce these.

Where two characters are required to be used, one can be typed with or over another by striking the first character, then the backspace key, then the second character. For upper-case characters the shift key is locked in position.

On manual machines it is sometimes necessary to use the variable line spacer to allow the characters to be raised or lowered slightly above or below the line of typing. Where half-line spacing is provided on the typewriter, this will be suitable for use as the necessary line (a half space up or down the page). However, the decimal point should not be raised above the line.

Electronic typewriters usually have some of the combination characters already incorporated into the top row numbers or at the side of the alpha keyboard. Check your own machine to see which of these you have.

The following list of combination characters and signs is arranged in alphabetical order and should be practised even if the typewriter being used has some of them.

Asterisk	*	Small **x** and hyphen raised half a space above the line of writing
Brace	(or)	Opening or closing brackets
Caret	/_	Oblique stroke and underscore
Cent	¢	Small **c** and oblique stroke
Dagger	†	Capital **I** and hyphen raised half a space above the line of writing
Dash	-	Hyphen preceded and followed by one space
Decimal point	3.5	Full stop on the line
Degrees	60°	Small **o** raised and close up to figure
Diaeresis	ü	Double quotes " over letter
Ditto	"	Double quotes
Division	÷	Colon : and hyphen -
Dollar	$	Capital **S** over oblique stroke /
Double dagger	‡	Two capital **I**'s
Equals sign	=	Hyphen and slightly raised hyphen
Exclamation mark	!	Apostrophe and full stop
Feet	12'	Apostrophe after figure
Fraction	61/16	Oblique stroke
Inches	9"	Double quotes " after figure

Minus	121 - 3	Hyphen preceded and followed by one space
Minutes	18'	Apostrophe after figure
Multiplication	4 x 5	Small **x** preceded and followed by one space
Seconds	30''	Double quotes '' after figure
Section mark	§	Small **s** over small **s** or capital **S** over capital **S**
Square bracket	[ ]	Oblique stroke and underscore

9

COPYING PRACTICE —— AND SPEED —— DEVELOPMENT

There has been graded practice on all four rows of the machine with the object of attaining keyboard mastery, but a good deal of supplementary copying practice will be necessary to complete that mastery. The sense of location will by now be fairly well developed, but regular daily copying practice will produce a noticeable improvement in accuracy and speed.

—————— Even margins ——————

The setting of the stop for the left-hand margin ensures evenness throughout, but the same perfection cannot be secured for the right-hand margin of typewritten work unless a machine with a justifying capability is being used.

In the earlier sections the exercises were arranged so that the right-hand margin finished at the same point of the scale, but normally this uniformity cannot be obtained. Evenness can, however, be achieved to a reasonable extent by using the hyphen for the division of words, although it should not be overdone. When used, the hyphen should be inserted at the end and not at the beginning of a line.

———— Division of words ————

General guidelines for the division of words are given below:

1 A word of one syllable or its plural should not be divided.
2 A word should not be divided so that only two letters remain at the end of a line or are carried forward to the next line.
3 A hyphenated word should only be divided at the existing hyphen.
4 Proper names and abbreviations should not be divided.
5 Dates should not be divided.
6 Serial numbers should not be divided.
7 A person's initials should not be separated from the surname – the forename should follow the title and may be separated in this instance from the surname.
8 A divided word should not end a paragraph or page.
9 A word should not be divided in such a way that pronunciation of either half is affected.
10 Words containing double consonants may usually be divided between those consonants.
11 Words containing three consecutive consonants may be divided after the first consonant.
12 Compound words may be divided at point of juncture.
13 A word may be divided after a prefix or before a suffix, provided that a two-letter division does not result.
14 Sums of money should not be divided.
15 If in doubt as to the correct point of division, do not divide.

When the bell gives warning of the approach of the end of the line of writing (usually six or eight spaces), a decision has to be made regarding the division of the word.

———— Line spacing ————

Standard typewriters generally provide for three depths of spacing between lines – *single-line spacing* (no space between the lines), *double-line spacing* (a depth of one blank line between each line of typewriting) and *treble-line spacing* (a depth of two line spaces between each line of typewriting). These three forms are shown in Exercise 21, and when

Exercise 21

Set margin stops at 30 and 66 (Elite type) and 25 and 60 (Pica type).
See page 47 for how to type underscore.

<u>Single-line spacing</u> is generally
used for long letters, invoices,
tabular statements, poetry,
synopses, footnotes, minutes
and lengthy documents. Between blocked
paragraphs, when using double-line
spacing, it is necessary to leave
one clear line space. (This is done
by setting the line space indicator
to 2 on manual machines, or by using
the RETURN key on electronic keyboards,
or cancelling the wordwrap facility on
the wordprocessor and pressing the
RETURN key accordingly.)

<u>Double-line spacing</u> is used for

short letters, lecture notes,

literary work, essays, sermons,

legal documents, dialogue in plays

and copy intended for the printer.

<u>Treble-line spacing</u> is used for

drafts, and for literary and legal

work which may need revision.

typing this the line space gauge should be properly adjusted for each depth of space and the line space lever operated to its fullest extent when returning the carriage to the right of the machine. The underscoring of the three items in the exercise will require the use of the shift lock. Here, the underscore is used for emphasis, and other uses for it are referred to on page 86.

—— Spacing after punctuation signs ——

The method of spacing recommended and adopted in the examples in this book is one space after a comma, colon or semicolon and two spaces after the full stop at the end of a sentence, and also after the exclamation mark and question mark. When using the hyphen as a dash sign, there should be a space left both before and after the dash. Also when quotation marks (or inverted commas ") and parentheses (or brackets both square and curved [] { }) are typed they should not be separated by any space from the words they enclose. Other methods of spacing are acceptable but, whichever style is decided upon (such as the 'house style' of a particular company), there must be consistency throughout the work. If, for example, three spaces are preferred after the full stop, this same break must be made after every sentence, exclamation mark and question mark.

Summary 2 spaces after . ! ?   1 space after , ; :

———————————— Underlining ————————————

The underlining device (found on manuals above the number 6, and on other electronic machines above the dash or other keys on the figure row) is used to underline individual letters, words or lines. It is sometimes referred to as the 'underscore'. It is used in emphasising important words for display work, foreign words and phrases, scientific terms, the names of authors at the end of quotations or notes, and to replace words typed which would normally be printed in italics.

When using the underlining device on a manual machine it should be set with the shift lock and the carriage returned with the platen knob to the exact point under which it is required to start to underline without use of the carriage return lever. On a wordprocessor use is made of an automatic underline command device instead. Underlining should not extend under a punctuation mark preceding or following the word or words to be emphasised.

Copying exercises

There is no need for the copying practice to be limited to the exercises given here, although these are carefully graded from easy material to more difficult. A section of any book, magazine or newspaper can be used for this purpose. It is useful to practise on a variety of material as this greatly improves speed, accuracy and extends ability.

Practice material is contained in the following exercises. The sentences need to be practised several times individually until a speedy and accurate copy is obtained. When you have decided that you have achieved a satisfying result at a fast rate, then progress to practising the paragraphs from page 62 onwards. These are graded to enable you to progress so that by the time you reach page 71 you will be able to copy from print any material you require. It is very helpful to read through the copy first, then decide on any particularly difficult words, practise these for several lines, followed by any words containing capital letters, or awkward phrases, and then progress to typing the whole paragraph. Where there is difficulty in typing any particular word, the word should be repeatedly typed until that particular letter combination can be copied at a fair rate of speed.

Do not be content with copying the complete exercise once only; each one should be copied several times as repetition of the correct action greatly helps skill and performance. Efforts should be made to slightly increase the speed of typing or keyboarding each time – *never put speed before accuracy but try to develop both together*. It is useful to remember that a little practice each day is much more beneficial than one long session once in a while!

Exercise 22

Practise each line until you – personally – are sure that you can type accurately and at reasonable speed.

They have arranged to forward this book by parcel post.

See a specialist before you agree to another operation.

We have now seen a full account of the new competition.

If they miss this train they will have an hour to wait.

Please use company letter headings for most of my mail.

They saw another book dealing with short story writing.

He had gone before we were able to check his signature.

During last week many of the men were not able to work.

Use of computers has increased the need to type faster.

We now have to learn foreign languages to visit Europe.

Set your own margin stops.

Exercise 23

A perfect copy is possible when you are a touch typist.

I am pleased to acknowledge the good work done by them.

We are having another machine at the end of the month.

They have taken the house and will be moving in August.

The retail price of butter will be increased next week.

Please co-operate with him as he is having a busy time.

If we add a form it will make a difference to the book.

There is now no doubt about the truth of their remarks.

It will be a pleasure for me to represent this company.

Please send him details of the "Teach Yourself" Series.

Exercise 24

An agenda is the list showing the order
and nature of the business to be
transacted at a meeting. Its preparation
is usually entrusted to the secretary
or to the person responsible for
convening the meeting.

Of all the various forms of written
communication used in organisations the
letter is by far the most common. It
provides an essential link between the
executives and departments of an
organisation and the many external
customers, associates and suppliers who
are necessary to the successful running
of either a business or government
department.

Public companies represent the largest
type of business organisation other than
those owned by the government. They are
composed of shareholders who are at
liberty to sell their shares publicly
without the consent of their fellow
shareholders.

In general, a director is one who has the
chief management of a scheme, design or
undertaking. More particularly, he is
one of a number of persons chosen by a
majority of the shareholders to conduct
the affairs of a company.

Exercise 25

Book-keeping is the technique of
keeping accounts, and recording in a
regular, concise and accurate manner
the financial transactions of a firm
in order to show the financial position
at any time.

Dividend is the proportion of profit
distributed to the shareholders as
a reward for investing in the company.
It is expressed either as an amount
per share or as a percentage of the
nominal value of each share.

An overdraft is the amount of cash
which a banker allows his customer
to draw out of his bank account in
excess of the total balance in the
customer's account.

An audit is the official examination
of the accounts of a firm to ensure
that they are kept in an accurate
manner. Laws require the regular
inspection of accounting records
by auditors.

The Bank of England was suggested by
William Paterson, a Scotsman, and it
received its charter of incorporation
in the year 1694. It was constituted
as a joint-stock company with a
capital of £1 200 000, that sum being
lent at interest to the Government
of the day.

Exercise 26

A good knowledge of at least one
European language is essential to
obtain the required competence in
Business Language skills. It is also
necessary to be able to use office
equipment in a practical situation.
Training involves acquisition of the
ability to deal, as a receptionist, with
visitors to offices, hotels, hospitals,
etc in an efficient, polite and
pleasant way.

Modern methods of efficient filing
depend on the storage of letters and
other documents to preserve them from
decay, dirt and damage and, to be easy to
use, they must be arranged according to
a plan which enables a speedy retrieval
afterwards. The plan to be followed must
be worked out in sufficient detail to
provide an exact and logical place for
each letter or document. Ease of
reference is just as important as
preservation from damage.

On the telephone a person's voice is an
important factor and has to stand on
its own merits without assistance from
any gestures or facial expressions.
Many people who appear to be gracious and
lucid in an ordinary conversation seem
surly and confused on the telephone.
All people who use the telephone should
study the faults they encounter at the
other end of the line and try, if possible,
to avoid these themselves.

Exercise 27

FAX is the term used to describe the system of facsimilie telegraphy. This means the instant transmission of printed or drawn items sent via a special copying device incorporated into telephone equipment. Companies are thus enabled to transmit any special letters, documents, photographs, diagrams, etc to many other FAX receivers all over the world as well as throughout Europe.

Business letters are produced today as the result of extensive teamwork. Firstly a graphics designer settles upon a suitable design for the organisation's letterheads. Next an office manager has to decide upon the colour and quality of the paper on which the letterhead will be printed. Many firms take a great deal of trouble over choosing the colours of the paper and letterhead designs and today desk-top publishing can be very helpful. In its final form a perfectly typed copy of the letter is produced on an electric typewriter or word processor, and this is then posted. Every discerning company knows that a good combination of design and attractive presentation will go a long way towards persuading the recipient of the letter to accept its message.

Whilst it is easier now to use the many books and visual aids such as posters in learning the spellings of various words, it is not always necessary to wait a whole year to have one's ability tested by an

Exercise 27 continued

examination. Now it is possible to learn
to spell correctly and to be tested at any
time by a range of officially verified
tests designed to help people judge their
own spelling ability. These cover either
general vocabulary or are particularly
designed for the specialist needs of such
areas as medicine or engineering.
This competence is part of the national
vocational training developments now
available and shows a person's individual
assets - very useful when seeking
suitable employment. Spelling test
achievements can now be listed amongst
qualifications in a curriculum vitae
of a person's educational achievements
and work experience.

Exercise 28

Many personal computers now allow the user to create 'formats' for letters, reports, labels and so on into which data from a document or datafile can be inserted. This is also extremely useful in preparing drafts of pages of books which can then be revised, improved and amended as the insertion of new material is easy. It is also nowadays an important asset to have an automatic spelling checker (or dictionary) which works by going through the pages and locating any word which has been misspelt. It then corrects the word. Even the most difficult words can be spelt correctly in this way, provided they already exist in the memory of the computer. Another attractive feature of modern computers is the choice of many different professional typestyles - some include flowing writing as an option for printing the final edited document.

---oOo---

A legal day is considered to be the whole of the day, continuing up to midnight. When there is a legal obligation to carry out a certain task by a fixed day, the whole day must pass before there can be a 'default'. For example, if rent is payable on a certain day then it is not in arrears until the following day.

---oOo---

Exercise 28 continued

An actuary is a person skilled in
calculating the value of life annuities
and insurances from tables of average
mortality rates worked out on mathematical
principles. He or she is also experienced
in the preparation of reports, etc in
connection with insurance matters generally
and his or her advice is called upon in
insurance claims arising from disasters,
especially where any increase in
subsequent premiums is possible.

---oOo---

Shipbrokers are agents - persons or
firms - in a seaport appointed by
shipowners to carry out and perform all
the necessary transactions connected with
the business of their vessels while
they are in harbour, such as entering and
clearing the vessels, collecting freight
and so on.

Exercise 29

Women have played a crucial literary role throughout history and there are many areas in which women's experiences are now the subject of books.

Women Heroines of the Second World War is a book which looks at the lives of ordinary women who fought alongside men in Europe, either in the resistance movements or at home in factories, and on the land. These brave women replaced men in dangerous jobs and often were in the firing line.

Another book has also recently been written about the many achievements of women as healers of all types - midwives, nurses, doctors and campaigners - and this is chronicled throughout the ages. Another has been written about Victorian women who worked down the coal mines and others who organised campaigns to defend the rights of women to work down the pits.

Books have also been written arguing that the suffrage movement, which resulted in women having the right to vote, helped the cause of democracy in Europe. This is affecting the woman of today in her search for equal job opportunity.

Yet another new book studies the text from women writers of the Middle Ages and pays tribute to their creative

Exercise 29 continued

talents, aspirations and emotional and
intellectual achievements.

Finally a Japanese writer produced a
masterpiece during the eleventh century
AD with her book - twice the length of
<u>War and Peace</u> - and this is still today
considered to be a first major work of
literature undertaken by a woman.

Exercise 30

The signs & (and) and @ (at) should never
be used in the body of a document as a
substitute for the word or words.
The ampersand (&) may only be used in
names of companies, street numbers and
abbreviations, and the @ sign may only
be used in accounts, invoices, price
lists or quotations. The per cent sign %
should only be used when immediately
following an arabic numeral.

10
—— PUNCTUATION ——

—— **Punctuation marks** ——

Correct punctuation is essential for the production of good typewritten work and should be studied carefully. The examples given below show some of the chief uses of the various punctuation marks, which are summarised in alphabetical order at the end of this chapter. Practise the 'typed' part of each section below.

Apostrophe (')

The apostrophe indicates ownership, a contraction or omission, or plurals of letters and figures. Type a single quotation mark.

Possessive singular – add an apostrophe and s ('s):

```
The BBC's programmes.
A typist's chair.
Mrs Brown's typewriter.
Mr Sandeman's desk.
Anderson's car.
SKY's and ITV's networks.
```

Possessive plural – add an apostrophe only:

```
Only seven days' notice is required.
Six months' leave was granted.
The girls' hats blew away.
Europe has plans for new theme parks'
   locations.
```

But if there is no 's' in the plural form, add one to form the possessive:

```
Men's clothes, children's holidays,
        machinery's power.
```

Possessive pronouns – do not require an apostrophe:

```
This is ours.  Where is yours?
The dog wagged its tail.  Theirs is in
the corner.  She has his and hers.
```

An apostrophe indicates the omission of a letter or letters:

```
        Don't  it's  can't
```

In plurals of abbreviations, letters and figures, the 's is added:

```
        There are two l's in Bell.
        You do not sound your t's.
        Two 2's are 4.
        There are many MP's here.
```

Capitals

Names of countries, continents, persons, months, days, places, book titles and so on are each written with an initial capital letter:

```
England  Scotland  Wales  France  Germany
Belgium  Holland  Italy  Spain  Greece
USA  Canada  Peru  China  Poland
Zambia  Romania  Hungary  Europe
Asia  Africa  India  Thomas Cook
W Shakespeare  Winston Churchill  February
March  December  May  Sunday  Monday
Tuesday  Wednesday  San Diego  New York
San Francisco  Rouen  St Helier  Brussels
Lisbon  Madrid  Cairo  Cape Town
Confravision  Prestel  Teletext  Datel
Telemessage  Voice mail  Videophone
Electronic Office  HM Customs  Post Office
Guide  Postal Rates  Overseas Compendium
Business Man's Guide  'Teach Yourself
Typing'  'Black Beauty'
```

Adjectives derived from proper names should be similarly treated:

```
Indian  French Revolution  American
             Japanese
```

There are some exceptions:

```
india rubber  french windows  french polish
```

Comma (,)

The comma denotes the shortest pause or break in continuity:

```
They live in houses, not in huts.
However, it has value.  Eurocheques, not
currency, are accepted here.  Mary, with
her head in her hands, wept profoundly.
```

Between two long phrases joined by 'and' the comma is often inserted:

```
We thank you for your letter, and have
pleasure in accepting the offer.
```

— **74** —

A short sentence of simple construction does not require commas:

```
I shall go there tomorrow.
```

Dash (–)

The dash may be used to indicate a break in a sentence. It is used also to separate items, eg the contents of chapters in books, and it precedes definitions, explanations and illustrations.

```
There are two kinds of spacing in
typewriting - character spacing and
line spacing.
```

When typing the dash leave one space before and one after.

Semicolon (;)

The semicolon indicates a pause in a sentence where the second clause is too closely linked to the first to justify complete separation:

```
There has been more than one postponement;
frequent consultations have taken place.
```

The semicolon is also used between clauses of compound sentences:

```
The girls attended the lectures on
fashions; the boys were not interested.
```

Colon (:)

The colon, although separating parts of a compound sentence, indicates continuity of thought:

```
Be careful how you act: actions speak
louder than words.
```

A longer pause is denoted by the colon rather than by the semicolon. Important uses of the colon are to introduce quotations, lists, summaries, and explanations:

The following books are recommended:
'Teach Yourself Mathematics', 'English
for Business', 'The Pitman Dictionary of
English and Shorthand', 'Teach Yourself
Word Processing'.

NB: The lists may be run on or typed in column form.

Full stop or period (.)

This mark is used to note the end of a complete sentence that is neither a
question nor an exclamation:

Please reply to our previous letter.

The full stop is also used as a decimal point and for time:

125.65   £4.20 $59.75   6.00 p.m.
20.45 hrs.

Full stops are not now used in modern open punctuation after abbreviations of words and people's names:

Dr T Merryweather Mrs B Stopford
Ms T Collins etc eg ie PS UK EEC
IMF AGM AD anon BSc BA Dept CO
Exors HMSO FAO IQ Jun km lb lit
lc O&M Messrs TT R/D

(A comprehensive list of abbreviations and their meanings is to be found
at the end of this book.)

Full stops are used in groups of three to denote omission of words –
this is called ellipses:

'Go to the shop ... and I'll wait
for you.'

Full stops are used in groups or continuously to guide the eye across a page and are called 'leader' dots. A minimum of one space must be left clear between the last preceding character and the first dot:

```
10 copies ... ... ... ... ... ... 120p
```

(See also page 79 – open and closed punctuation.)

Emphasis

The underscore can be used to emphasise a particular expression:

```
We shall require copies not later than
Wednesday next.
```

Hyphen (-)

This may show the relationship of two or more words forming a compound word:

```
half-length self-contained self-confident
over-weight over-enthusiastic touch-type
touch-and-go change-over shorthand-typist
follow-up Desk-top Publishing
```

The hyphen is also used to mark division of a word at the end of the line of writing, the remainder being carried to the beginning of the next line. Word processors of course do not split words in this way because of the word wrap facility previously described.

Nowadays, the tendency is to use the hyphen as seldom as possible and many words which were formerly hyphenated (eg co-operate) are now written as one word (cooperate).

Question mark (?)

This is used after a direct question:

```
What is the price of the portable
typewriter?
How much shall we pay for a new portable
computer?
```

A question mark is not necessary when an order is given in the form of a question:

```
Will you kindly let us have the
information as soon as possible.
```

Parenthesis ()

This is used to enclose subsidiary words, clauses or sentences to explain the leading idea of the sentence:

```
The order (No 3) to which you refer
has now been completed.
Tinted typewriting papers (usually of
a cheaper quality) are used for
specialised copies.
```

Square brackets [] are used to make further enclosure within a parenthesis, and also for specialised and legal work.

Parenthesis should be used sparingly to avoid awkward sentences.

Quotation marks (' ' or " ")

Quotation marks are used to enclose words exactly as quoted:

```
'I wish,' he said, 'to express my
gratitude.'
```

The quotation mark should not be placed at the beginning of every line of quoted paragraphs, but only before the first word of each paragraph and at the end of the complete quotation.

The choice of single or double quotation marks is optional but the style adopted should be used consistently. When a citation occurs within a citation, the alternative form should be used to avoid confusion.

NB: the signs ampersand (&) and @ (at) should never be used in the body of a document as a substitute for the word or words. The ampersand (&) may only be used in names of companies, street numbers and abbreviations, and the sign @ may only be used in accounts, invoices, price lists or quotations. The per cent sign % should only be used when immediately following an arabic number.

—— Open and closed punctuation ——

The method of typewriting which uses a minimum of punctuation is known as open punctuation. This speeds up and simplifies the typist's work, and is most apparent in the omission of full stops after abbreviations. The following comparisons show how punctuation marks may be omitted without any loss of clarity.

Open punctuation

```
We shall expect you at 9 am on Thursday.
Mr J T Smith BSc FRSA
Harry works in the USA.
Please check in at 1500 hrs on Sunday.
Sell all the furniture, ie the tables
  and chairs.
This can be paid at any SWEB shop.
PS  Greece is a member of the EEC.
HRH The Princess of Wales.
Bring all your old toys, etc, to the sale.
```

Closed punctuation

```
We shall expect you at 9 a.m. on Thursday.
Mr. J. T. Smith, B.Sc., F.R.S.A.
Harry works in the U.S.A.
Please check in at 15.00 hrs. on Sunday.
Sell all the furniture, i.e. the tables
  and chairs.
This can be paid at any S.W.E.B. shop.
P.S.  Greece is a member of the E.E.C.
H.R.H. The Princess of Wales.
Bring all your old toys, etc., to the
  sale.
```

Since open punctuation is now widely accepted, most of the typed examples in the book will follow this style. Whichever method is chosen, however, it is important to show consistency within a single piece of work.

—— Punctuation summary ——

How to type and when to use

Apostrophe   indicates ownership, omission, contraction or plurals of letters and figures (use single quotation mark when typing – ')

Capitals   use individual shift key and release before typing rest of word. Can also be used with shift lock for closed capitals, eg names of persons, months, days, places, book titles, abbreviations such as BBC, ITV, EEC, USA, UNESCO, PTO, STD, PO, PS, RSVP, O/D, MC, MP, IQ, IMP, HMSO, ETA, etc plus adjectives from proper names, eg French Revolution, Indian Mutiny, (but not french windows, india rubber)

Closed punctuation — a style of typing which uses full stops after sentences, abbreviations, and uses full punctuation in addressee's name and address

Colon (see also dash) — separates parts of a compound sentence but on same theme (leave one space after typing colon)

Comma — denotes shortest pause or break, and used when joining two long phrases (leave one space after typing comma)

Dash — used to indicate a break in a sentence and to split items, used for contents of chapters, or used to precede definitions (always leave one clear space before and after dash)

Emphasis — use underlining device (underscore) to ensure that attention is drawn to particular word or phrase

Exclamation mark — as at the end of sentences – denotes expression of a wish, emotion, or remarkable event

Full stop — used to note the end of a complete sentence that is neither question nor exclamation. Also used as decimal point (typed on line but *not* raised above line), and as ellipses to indicate omission of words (use spaced dots . . . or closed dots ...)

Hyphen — hyphen has no space either side of it and shows two words forming compound word, or used to divide words at line endings (now not used very much)

Open punctuation — an open style of typing which uses a minimum of punctuation. This is speedily achieved and uses no full stops after abbreviations, no commas in names, nor in addresses for addresses etc (see also p. 91)

Parenthesis — brackets are used next to the portion required to be in brackets – in addition if second bracket required draw or use { } [ ]

Question mark — this is used after a direct question – found in various positions on keyboard, sometimes needs use of individual shift

Quotation mark can use single '.....' for conversation and for quoting reports of what is actually said; marks must be placed at beginning of first word of each paragraph and then finally *only* at the end of the typing of the complete quotation (same use for double "..." quotation marks)

Semicolon use when the second part (clause) of a sentence is closely linked to the first part

11

BUSINESS LETTERS, ENVELOPE ADDRESSING AND MEMORANDA

——————— Business letters ———————

The letter is by far the most common form of written communication used by organisations, and these letters will convey their messages more effectively if they are attractively produced.

The chief characteristics of a good letter are clearness, accuracy, brevity and courtesy. There are various components of a business letter, and in the paragraphs that follow each part is explained in full, ie letter headings, references, date, name and address of addressee (person or firm to whom the letter is being sent), salutation (Dear Sir, etc.), subject heading (if any), body of the letter, continuation sheets (if necessary), complimentary close, title (designation) of the sender (if any), enclosures and envelopes.

For your own portfolio you may wish to include some of the business letters given at the end of this chapter as examples that you have personally typed.

Sizes of letter paper

The standard size is A4 (210mm = 297mm = 8¼in × 11¾in). For very short letters and private (personal) correspondence you can use A5 size (210mm × 148mm = 5⅞in × 8¼in). Both sizes can be used in either portrait style or landscape style.

A4 and A5
Portrait style ↕

A4 and A5
Landscape style ↔

Letter headings

These headings are generally the product of the graphics designer and printer, and are carefully prepared since they play an important part in projecting the desired corporate image. The details given in the letter heading include, in bold display type, the name and business of the firm, the company's registered address from which that business is conducted, company number (as applicable), telephone, telex and/or FAX numbers, etc. For private correspondence the letter heading usually only contains the address and telephone number.

Width of margins

Margin widths are governed largely by individual preference and the length of the letter, and the margin stops should be set before commencing work. A minimum left margin of 25mm (1in) is generally recommended for A4 paper, however, with a slightly narrower margin for A5.

Modern practice is to allow even left and right margins to secure a centred effect on the paper, in much the same way as the printed page of a book.

Insertion of date

The order recommended is day, month (spelled out in full) and year typed on one line, as:

```
17 April 19--  or 17th April, 19--
```

Commence the date at the left-hand margin point when adopting the fully blocked style, and let it finish flush with the right-hand margin when using the indented or semi-blocked style of layout.

Reference initials

In business correspondence these references usually consist of the initials of the dictator and the typist, as **DF/OH** or **DF/oh**. Alternatively, a departmental number may be used, as **SALES/916**. If a place has not been allotted for these details in the printed letter heading, they can be placed at the left-hand margin, as shown in the examples on pages 91 and 98. Sometimes the initials are inserted at the end of the letter. When replying to a correspondent, do not forget to include his or her reference. It will be helpful to him or her in dealing with the letter – that is the reason for its insertion.

Attention line

When instructions are given that correspondence must be addressed to a firm and not to individuals, it is common practice to insert an attention line reading.:

```
FOR THE ATTENTION OF MR J HARMAN
```

two line spaces above the inside address (see pages 86 and 94).
For the layout of an attention line on an envelope, see page 94.

Inside name and address

The name and address of the person or firm to whom the letter is being sent are in most cases placed at the beginning of the letter. Single-line spacing should be used, with all lines beginning at the left-hand margin point. It is common practice to type the inside address in the same form as the envelope address (see pages 92–94), with the post town in capital letters.

Every care should be taken to ensure that the name of the correspondent is given correctly.

Personal, private, confidential

When it is desired for a specific reason to restrict the reading of the letter to one particular person, the words giving the instruction should be typed, preferably in capitals, two line spaces above the inside address.

Salutation

The opening to a letter is termed the 'salutation', and the most common forms used include:

```
Dear Sir    Dear Mrs Jones   Dear Mr Smith
Dear Sirs   Dear Madam       Dear Ms Black
```

Type the salutation two or three line spaces below the inside address.

Subject heading

When a subject heading is required it should be typed two line spaces below the salutation and may be typed at the left-hand margin point or centred over the writing line. Unless the heading ends with an abbreviation, a full stop should not be inserted after it. A heading typed in lower case with initial capitals should preferably be underscored.

Body of letter

This contains the subject matter of the letter. It should commence two line spaces below the subject heading, or two line spaces below the salutation if there is no heading. Paragraphs may be blocked or indented according to the letter style. Single-line spacing with double-line spacing between paragraphs is preferable, but double-line spacing throughout is sometimes used for very short letters of one paragraph.

Do not use the ampersand (&) for 'and' in the body of the letter, unless reference is made to the name of a firm or street numbers are being quoted.

Insets

These are paragraphs that are displayed within the body of the letter. If the paragraphs are numbered or lettered, two or three spaces should be left after the number or letter or its closing bracket.

Inset paragraphs may be blocked, indented or 'hanging'. When the blocked method of layout is being used, 'inset' matter can begin at the left-hand margin. Otherwise, paragraphs should be indented equally from both margins. In 'hanging' paragraphs the first line overhangs the second and subsequent lines by two spaces.

Double-line spacing should always be used between the text and the inset material, and, unless the items are very short, between paragraphs in the portion inset.

Continuation sheets

These are necessary when a letter occupies more than one sheet of paper, and they should be of the same size and quality as the letter heading. Continuation sheets are not usually printed with the firm's letter heading. The details required on the continuation sheet are the page number, the date and the addressee.

When the fully blocked style of letter layout is used, the details are listed separately at the left-hand margin:

```
2
17 April 19--
R Kelly Esq
```

With the indented method, the information is evenly displayed across one line with the page number in the centre:

```
R. Kelly, Esq.  (2) 17th April, 19--
```

Do not use a continuation sheet for only two lines. A readjustment of margins may make it possible to type the letter on one sheet.

Complimentary close

This is typed two line spaces below the final paragraph of the letter and should begin at the left-hand margin point or the middle of the line of writing. Those most used are:

```
Yours sincerely  Yours truly
        Yours faithfully
```

The form of complimentary close should match the salutation – 'Yours faithfully' with 'Dear Sir' but 'Yours sincerely' with 'Dear Mr Smith'.

Name of the firm or company

Capital letters are used if the name of the company follows the complimentary close, and the letter may be signed by a member of the staff who acts as an agent.

The name of the company may be prefaced by the word 'for'. The abbreviated form of *per procurationem* – **per pro.** or **p. p.** – is also used.

The signature

This will be handwritten, and, when the designation of the writer is placed after the complimentary close, a minimum of five line spaces should be left for the insertion of the signature. The designation should be typed at the left-hand margin point, or be centred under, or commence at the same point as, the complimentary close when the indented or semi-blocked style of layout is employed.

Enclosures

The indication of enclosures to a letter is given by typing the abbreviated form **Enc** or **2 Encs** in the space that may be provided for this information or at the bottom left-hand corner of the letter. (If there is room, **Enc** should be typed two or three line spaces below the designation.) Labels are sometimes affixed to the letter and a duplicate placed on the enclosure.

Another method of showing enclosures is to type three dots or hyphens in the margin on the same line as the reference to an enclosure.

Carbon copying

For business transactions it is desirable to have a record of documents despatched, and there are various methods of copying letters, etc. That most popular is the carbon-paper method; the copies are made at the same time as the original. The number of copies that can be secured by this means will depend upon the typewriter used and the quality of the typewriting paper.

Normally carbon paper can be obtained in a variety of sizes and colours, and single-sided carbons (coated on one side) are mostly used.

In preparing to take carbon copies, the first sheet should be placed face downwards on the table. On this a sheet of carbon paper should be placed, with the coated surface upwards; then another sheet of paper, another carbon and so on for the required number. See that the carbon sheets are in correct position so that all the original appears on the copies.

When the sheets are inserted in the machine, care should be taken to see that the coated side of the sheet faces the cylinder, and the pressure of the feed rolls should be released by depressing the paper release lever, particularly when there are several sheets. The pressure can be restored when the top edges of the sheets have passed the feed rolls. This pressure should also be released when the sheets are withdrawn from the machine.

It is usual to identify the recipient of a carbon copy on the original, by typing the name on the same line as the letters **cc**. Sometimes, however, a *blind carbon copy* (bcc) may be required – perhaps for a colleague, for

Example of a fully blocked business letter

Remember to start with each line at the left-hand margin

L E T T E R H E A D I N G
Name & address of firm plus
telephone and FAX numbers

Line space:

1		
	Our ref	uses initials of writer, oblique / then typist
0		eg HM/LK
	Your ref	eg LMS/DFB
1		
	Date	Day, month in words and then year eg 7 March 199-
1		
	Any special instructions	PERSONAL, PRIVATE & CONFIDENTIAL, URGENT, FOR THE ATTENTION OF
1		
	Name and address of addressee	Start at margin for fully blocked, use fresh line for post town in CAPS. Post code is on last line - 1 space between 2 parts of code, eg Miss L M Sewell 56 Bell Lane EASTBOURNE BN21 1LJ
1		
	Salutation	Dear ...
1		
	Subject heading	USE UPPER CASE AND/OR BOLD - NO UNDERSCORE or USE lower case words underscored
1		
	Body of letter	Always leave one clear line between paragraphs
1		
	Complimentary close	eg Yours faithfully (goes with Dear Sir) Yours sincerely (goes with Dear Mr, Miss)
0	Name of firm	(if applicable), eg Yours faithfully JOHNSON & SONS PLC
4		
	Name of person signing letter Title of person	Sometimes Mr, Miss, Ms is put after name, eg Helen Miller (Miss) eg Managing Director
1		
	Enc	No full stop in open punctuation

Example of an open-punctuated fully blocked style, with subject heading.

```
                    W R I T E R S   I N   S T Y L E
                              P L C
                        WESTBOURNE HOUSE
                         BUSHEY HEATH
                        Herts      WD2 56PY

    Telephone 08100950 005778        FAX 08100950 005888
    (2)
    Our ref     HM/LK
    Your ref    LMS/DFB
    (2)
    7 March 199-
    (2)
    PERSONAL
    (2)
    Miss L M Sewell
    56 Bell Lane
    EASTBOURNE
    BN21 1LJ
    (2)
    Dear Madam
    (2)
    FULLY BLOCKED BUSINESS OR PERSONAL LETTERS
    (2)
    I am writing to let you know how easy it is to obtain
    a neat, efficient appearance in any business or
    personal letter by using the above fully blocked style
    of display.
    (2)
    You will see that one line space is left between the
    reference, date, special instruction line, addressee's
    name and address and the salutation, etc.  in fact
    the only place that there is need for more space to
    be left is when typing the complimentary close and
    the name of the person signing the letter (called the
    signatory).  You need to leave four clear line spaces
    for the signature.  Finally, one clear line is left
    between the title of the person and any enclosure to
    be sent with the letter.
    (2)
    I hope that you will find this information as useful
    as I did when I started typing business letters.
    I also enclose one of our brochures on 'New Job
    Opportunities in Writing' which I think you will enjoy
    reading.
    (2)
    Yours faithfully
    WRITERS IN STYLE PLC
    (5)
    Helen Miller  (Miss)
    Managing Director
    (2)
    enc
```

Note: The numbers between the parts of the letter show the number of lines to turn up.

information – in which case the letters **bcc** and the recipient's name or designation are typed on the carbon(s) only, and not on the original.

Correction on carbon copies

One method of correction is to place a small piece of paper between each carbon and its copy at the point where the erasure is to be made. First make the erasure on the top copy; next lift the first carbon and remove the small piece of paper and erase the error from the carbon copy; then lift the second carbon and follow the same procedure until all the copies have been dealt with. Before typing the correction all the pieces of paper must be removed.

Carbon economy

Wastage of carbon sheets can be avoided by reversing them immediately there is sign of wear, the bottom carbon being placed at the top for subsequent copies.

Layout

On page 90 the suggested layout for an open punctuated, fully blocked letter is given in diagrammatic form, together with a key to the sections. On page 91 an example of an open punctuated, fully blocked letter with subject heading is given. You will find, however, when working in an office, that the company has its own decided views and rules on house-style with regard to spacings, layout and so on.

——— Envelope addressing ———

When typing envelopes it is necessary to remember to include:

Person or company name	Miss L A H Owens
House number, building name (if any), street	29 Birchwood Mews
local description of area (if supplied)	Whitstone
TOWN NAME (in BLOCK CAPS)	TALGARTH
County (in lower case with initial cap)	Brecon
Postcode	LD3 O68
Country	Wales

The usual guide on where to begin typing an envelope is to commence about halfway down from the top edge so as to leave 1½ inches for postage stamps and a postmark. Indent from the left-hand side approximately 1½ inches to 2 inches, the name and address being roughly centred. It is useful to put a light pencil dot to indicate where you need to start typing but no measurements are necessary. Almost all companies now incorporate fully blocked style into addresses (see examples below).

Note that except for large towns like London the county is included on a separate line and the Post Office also prefer the postal code to be on a separate line.

Commonly used sizes for envelopes:
C 6 (114 mm × 162 mm)
C5/6 (110 mm × 222 mm)

Addresses are usually typed in single spacing, but double spacing may be used for large envelopes or if the address is very short.

Courtesy titles, such as *Mrs, Mr, Dr, Ms, The Rev*, etc should always be included with the name. *Messrs* is sometimes used when addressing a partnership, except when the name of the firm is preceded by the word *The* or a title is included (examples: *Messrs Brown & Jones, Messrs Avis & Co*, but *The Regent Manufacturing Co, Sir James Smith & Co*). A limited company, however, is an incorporated body – a legal person, distinct from any of its members – so that *Messrs* is strictly out of place when used before the name of a limited company, although if personal names are included, *Messrs* is sometimes used in practice.

Initials representing first names should always be followed by a space, but degrees and complimentary initials after a name, such as *MA, BSc, MBE*, are not divided by a space.

Supplementary notes placed on the envelope, such as *Personal, Urgent*, etc, should be typed two line spaces above the name. Internal instructions, such as *First Class*, may be typed in the top left-hand corner.

When *Junior* and *Senior* are required (father and son with the same first name and at the same address) the abbreviations (*Jun* or *Sen*) are placed immediately after the name, as *Mr Arthur Carey Jun* or *Arthur Carey Jun Esq*.

Examples of addresses are given below, and in Exercise 31 a list of names and addresses (all fictitious) are provided for practice. A folded sheet of paper, or any scrap of paper with an area similar to an ordinary envelope, will be suitable for practice. The reverse side of the front of any used envelope also provides good working paper.

Examples of block form of address

```
            Sir James Brown & Sons Ltd
            345 Rochester Road
            CHATHAM
            Kent
            CH9 2SB
```

```
            FOR THE ATTENTION OF MR. J. SMITH

            Messrs. James Melhish & Co. Ltd.,
            546 Caledonian Road,
            BIRMINGHAM.
            B9 5TX
```

(Note that in this address the punctuation is 'closed')

Exercise 31

Type the following address in block form with open punctuation.

Dr John Laughton, 36 Dudley Road, Derby
    DE6 2LX
Messrs S W Kemp & Sons, 26-30 Booth
    Street, Northampton NN5 5LT
Mr Robert Macdonald, 145 Ladywood Road,
    Portsmouth PO1 5RJ
Major Herbert Wilson DSO, Bridge Avenue,
    Reading, Berks RG4 OA2
Professor Sir Albert Lawrence, Melville
    Lodge, Coventry CV1 3AN

   (Show that the letter is confidential)

J N C Allerton Esq, 29 Whitmore Road,
    Plymouth PL3 5LU
E Griffiths & Co Ltd, Exeter Street,
    Newmarket NE7 1NJ
Ms W Odell, 63 Charlton Hill, Chester
    CH1 4JN
Mrs A Freeman, J Freeman & Sons Ltd,
    Compton Road, Bournemouth BH8 9NG

   (Show that the letter is personal)

Mr Robert Grant Jun, Belmont Road,
    Falmouth FA9 2XC
F T Pemberton & Co Ltd, 42-48 Ashley Road,
    Dover, Kent DO9 6SP
The Rev William Gardner MA, The Rectory,
    Grange Road, Norwich NO8 5RM

Type the following addresses in block form with closed punctuation.

The Bridge Manufacturing Co. Ltd.,
    Claremont Road, Gloucester. GL1 5PH
Mrs. Elsie Davidson, 29 Stapleton Road,
    Greenwich, London. SE13 5NB

Memorandums

The memorandum is used for internal communications only, ie between members of the same organisation. A memorandum (or memo) form is usually A5 (landscape), although A4 may be used for longer memos. The heading 'Memorandum' is printed or typed at the top of the page. There is no salutation or closure, but spaces are provided for the sender's and recipient's designations or names, the date, and possibly the reference and subject. Care should be taken to ensure that the typed details are lined up with the printed headings. The subject heading may be typed at the left-hand margin or centred or inserted in the space provided. A left-hand margin of 25 mm (1 inch) should be allowed, unless the memo is aligned with the printed matter at the top, which may be less than 25 mm from the edge of the paper.

Specimen layout for a memorandum

```
                    M E M O R A N D U M

        To Sales Representative
        From Buying Manager                 3 October 19--




        CHRISTMAS NOVELTIES
        The new catalogue of Christmas Novelties is now
        available.  Please let me know as soon as possible
        how many copies you will require for distribution
        to your customers.




        EMW/JW
```

— Linked themes —

On the following pages there are examples of business letters, memoranda and personal business letters. These are incorporated into sets of correspondence on linked themes. The theme is a set of correspondence between various people and firms linked by a logical progressive sequence of events.

Exercise 32

Layout of internal memorandum

Example of an open-punctuation fully-blocked style memorandum with heading. Compose your own reference and add at end of page.

M E M O

```
TO          All staff
(2)
FROM        Managing Director
(2)
DATE        23 August 199-
(2)
SUBJECT     SPOT THE ERROR COMPETITION PRIZEWINNER
(2)
```
We have now scrutinised all the entries for the above
competition - we received 239,327 in all - and found
that only one person correctly located the 1,439
errors in the manuscript. This is Miss B L Cross and
I have today written to notify her and to send her
the cheque for £12,000.
(2)
There will naturally be a release to the Press
concerning our winner and I am holding the special
Press Conference on Monday at 1100 hours. Everyone
should be present to maximise the coverage and I need
not stress to you all that Miss Cross's home address
and telephone number must be kept entirely confidential.
From a telephone conversation I had with her, I
gather she plans shortly to have a holiday in Devon
with a friend who has been ill, and after that to go
abroad (following the official presentation) which may
help her to avoid the inevitable considerable
publicity.
(2)
Thank you all for your help in what has been - for
this Company - a most worthwhile competition. We
raised a total of £120,000 for the WWW Fund, and the
Company has been personally thanked by the European
President of that Fund.

Exercise 33

Layout of a fully blocked letter

Example of an open-punctuation fully blocked style letter with heading.
Instructions – Choose suitable margins and type a copy of this business letter.
             – Type an envelope.

W O R L D   W I D E   P U B L I S H I N G   P L C

MASON'S COURT CROMWELL WAY
BIRMINGHAM BM5 9WS

TELEPHONE 021 2789 453576   **FAX 021 2789 426354**

Your ref
Our ref   BLC/23/ED

23 August 199-

Miss B L Cross
22 Little Heath Close
Muswell Hill
LONDON
N10 8UK

Dear Miss Cross

COMPETITION PRIZE – TENTH ANNIVERSARY
We are writing to inform you that you have been
awarded first prize in our SPOT THE ERROR competition
run in conjunction with the Medwater Publishing
Company, and commemorating our Tenth Anniversary
as publishers.

Your entry correctly located the 1,439 errors in the
manuscript of the book published and entitled 'Keep
the World Greener'. Yours was the only entry that
successfully detected <u>all</u> the deliberate mistakes.
We wish to congratulate you on this outstanding
achievement and enclose cheque for £12,000 made out
in your name. Please acknowledge and return our
official receipt in the enclosed self-addressed
envelope.

We hope that you will be able to fulfill some life-
long ambition by winning this competition.

Our publicity department will wish to take some
photographs of you, with your permission, and will be
contacting you shortly.

Yours sincerely
WORLD WIDE PUBLISHING PLC

Managing Director

encs

Exercise 34

Instructions – Use A5 plain paper (landscape) for following:
  – Attach receipt to letter to Miss B L Cross.

```
R E C E I P T

TO WORLD WIDE PUBLISHING PLC
(in conjunction with MEDWATER PUBLISHING CO)

I HEREBY ACKNOWLEDGE RECEIPT OF CHEQUE FOR £12,000
(TWELVE THOUSAND POUNDS) BEING THE SUM AWARDED TO ME
FOR FIRST PRIZE IN THE TENTH ANNIVERSARY COMPETITION.


Signed .........................

Date ..................19..

(Belinda L Cross)
```

Read through the rest of the series of linked correspondence in this section, then type perfect copies of each as follows:

Exercise 34: Letter from Miss Cross to her friend Miss Daphne Mortimer.

Exercise 35: Letter from Miss Cross to the Managing Director of World Wide Publishing PLC thanking him for sending the cheque.

Exercise 36: Letter from Miss Cross to Mr W Richardson, Bank Manager of Barcham's Bank PLC concerning investment of money.

Exercise 37: Mr Richardson's reply to Miss Cross.

Exercise 38: Memo from Mr Richardson to Kevin Millhouse.

Remember:
● in each letter or memo you must choose your own suitable margins and ensure that A4 sized paper is used unless specific instructions are given to the contrary;
● this correspondence must be mailable (ie free from errors) and ready for signature in each case.

Exercise 35

Instructions – This is an example of *indented* style of letter.
Note also the alternative position of the addressee's name and
address. You may also omit the addressee's name and address in
personal letters of this type.
– Set a tab half an inch from left hand margin.
– Type an envelope.

---

                                        22 Little Heath Close
                                        Muswell Hill
                                        LONDON   N10 8UK

Telephone 091 080 749   2 September 199.

Dear Daphne

    I am writing to let you know the good news that I
have just received from World Wide Publishing PLC.

    As you may remember, I entered a competition in
their magazine to spot the manuscript errors in an
author's book which was shortly to be published. It
was all about the environment and was entitled
'Keep the World Greener'. The Company has just
written to say that I have won First Prize and they
also enclosed their cheque for £12,000!

    The first thing I have decided to do is to pay for
a holiday in California for both of us. I know that
when I went there with Jane and Thelma last year
you would have been very eager to come if you had
been able to do so. This is now your chance to see
America. As you have been so exhausted since that
last bout of influenza, I think a few days away in
Devon in the very near future will be a tonic for
both of us.

    Shall I go ahead and book the flights and accommodation
for San Diego and a suitable hotel on Exmoor? We
can easily manage this year to stay in a five-star
hotel. Please telephone to let me know your decision
as soon as possible, and send a list of convenient
dates for the holidays.

    Best wishes

            Yours sincerely

Miss Daphne Mortimer
67 Tether Lane
Crews Hill
ENFIELD
Middx

Exercise 36

Instructions – Choose suitable margins and type a copy of this letter.
                 – Type an envelope.

---

                                                 22 Little Heath Close
                                                 Muswell Hill
                                                 LONDON

Telephone 091 080 749   N1O 8UK

Your ref   BLC/23/ED

2 September 199-

The Managing Director
World Wide Publishing PLC
Mason's Court
Cromwell Way
BIRMINGHAM   BM5 9WS

Dear Sir

COMPETITION PRIZE - TENTH ANNIVERSARY

Thank you for your letter of the 23 August 19..
informing me that I have won first prize in the above
and enclosing your Company's cheque for £12,000.
I now return your official receipt, which I have duly
signed and dated.

I am extremely grateful to your Company for so kindly
organising this competition in aid of the World
Well-Animal Wildlife Fund. The fact that I have won
first prize will enable me to help a friend who has
been ill to benefit from two exciting holidays in
the near future.

I have no objection to my photograph being given
to the Press.

Yours faithfully

Belinda L Cross (Miss)

enc

Exercise 37

Instructions – Choose suitable margins and type a copy of this letter.
– Type an envelope.

---

                                        22 Little Heath Close
                                        Muswell Hill
                                        LONDON   N10 8UK

Telephone 091 080 749

Your ref KG/RTD/2998/wr/ls

16 September 199-

Mr W Richardson
Barcham's Bank PLC
High Street
ELMS END
Cambs
CB3 1DR

Dear Mr Richardson

I am writing to enquire whether you could help me
with some investment advice.

Recently I have been fortunate enough to win a
considerable sum of money as a result of entering and
winning the Spot the Error Competition held in aid
of the WWW Fund. I now need to have some advice on
how to invest this in an appropriate account to give
the maximum return each month. As I shall be using
some of the money for a holiday in the USA, I will
also need to order some travellers' cheques and
currency from your bank.

Can you tell me please how much notice you require
for currency (dollars) and for travellers' cheques
to be prepared?

An early reply from you will be much appreciated as
I plan to leave for the USA around 25 October.

Yours sincerely

Belinda L Cross (Miss)

Exercise 38

BARCHAM'S BANK PLC

HIGH STREET
ELMS END CAMBS CB3 1DR

Telephone: 0353 666882   Fax: 0344 78934

Our ref KG/RTD/2998/wr/ls

18 September 199-

Miss B L Cross
22 Little Heath Close
Muswell Hill
London   N1O 8UK

Dear Miss Cross

Thank you for your letter of 16 September concerning
investment possibilities.

I was very pleased to hear about your admirable
success in winning the competition and I am sure that
it must have taken a great deal of skill to detect
all the errors in that manuscript. It so happens
that I also endeavoured to discover them when the
competition was run and only succeeded in finding
about 800! From what I have just read in the Press,
you discovered 1,439 which was excellent.

1)   I am enclosing a brochure of our latest profile
     plan which I am sure you will find interesting.
     I am also asking our Securities expert, Kevin
     Millhouse, to prepare a special set of options
     for you to look at including any tax free
     investments that you may wish to make.

2)   Perhaps you would be good enough to look through
     the enclosed papers and also discuss the set of
     options with Kevin Millhouse. Afterwards you
     can book an appointment to discuss in detail
     with me what you have decided to do.

3)   As regards your holiday, the bank requires only
     a minimum of three working days for the ordering
     of currency but we do keep travellers' cheques
     in stock all the time, so you can obtain these
     when you collect your currency.

Yours sincerely

Manager
enc

Exercise 39

Instructions – Choose *suitable* margins and type a copy of this fully blocked
  memo.
  – Produce a *copy* of the memo either on a photocopier or use carbon
  paper.
  – Include reference WR/KG/RTD/2998.
  – Use your own template or copy the one below.

M E M O

TO   Kevin Millhouse Securities

FROM   William Richardson

DATE   17 September 199-

SUBJECT   CLIENT INVESTMENT ADVICE

I have been asked by one of our clients to provide an
investment portfolio for a considerable sum of
money which she wishes to invest to obtain maximum
return on capital. I thought you would be able to
arrange a plan for her. Looking at my records I
find that she is 39 years old and anticipates
retiring at age 60.

When I telephoned this client she informed me that
she intends to invest about £8,500. Are there any
tax-free investments that she can make?

Please look upon this as a matter of urgency as she
is going on holiday in October.

12

FORMS, AGENDAS __ AND MINUTES

In this chapter various typewritten examples are reproduced, and they provide additional copying practice. Where the examples contain blank spaces for the later insertion of details, it is suggested that one or two copies be made so that the typist can practise filling in different details on the same original.

——————— Postcards ———————

These are used for business or personal correspondence when the message to be conveyed is short. The recipient's address is typed on the front and the message on the reverse side. Most business firms have their name and address printed on their postcards, but a typed address should be confined to one line if possible and may be separated from the text by a continuous line. As in the case of memos, there is no salutation or closure. Postcards are normally A6 (148 mm × 105 mm) and margins of 1.5 cm (½ in) to 2.5 cm (1 in) should be allowed depending on the length of the message.

Specimen layout for a postcard

```
"ALLCLEAN" 9 HIGH STREET HITCHIN HERTS  SG5 9PY

EWW/12                              3 November 19--

We are pleased to inform you that your curtains
are now awaiting collection.

                              Manager
```

```
                    POST CARD




        Mrs J Curtis
        19 Bell Close
        HITCHIN
        Herts
        SG4 9PG
```

Forms

Application forms, enrolment forms, questionnaires, etc, should have an adequate number of lines for the information requested. The lines should be double-spaced to provide enough room or the details to be filled in later, and should be typed either with the underscore or the full stop. Not all lines will necessarily be the same length: while an address may require two or three lines, other items such as telephone number or nationality may need only a small space. One space should be left before the lines begin after a word and before another word appearing on the same line.

Specimen layout for a form

```
          FURTHER EDUCATION TEACHER'S CERTIFICATE

          RSA TEFL    *a)  Preparatory Certificate
                       b)  Final Certificate

                       * Delete as necessary

     APPLICATION

     Miss)
     Mrs ) ............... Forenames ...................
     Mr  )

     Date of birth .................

     Address ...........................................

     ...................................................

     ............................. Tel no ...........

     Date ............... Signature ..................
```

Filling in forms

When filling in forms it is necessary to type over lines which may be dotted or continuous and the paper should be adjusted by using the variable line spacer. No character should cut through a line and care should be taken to see that the 'tailed' letters – **g**, **j**, **p**, **q** and **y** – just clear it. At the same time the typed characters should not 'fly' more than half a line space above the line. It may be necessary to re-align each line of typing if the lines have not previously been produced on a typewriter.

Deletions may be made by a lower or upper case **X** or hyphen.

A completed form

FURTHER EDUCATION TEACHER'S CERTIFICATE

RSA TEFL   *a)   Preparatory Certificate
            b)   ~~Preparatory Certificate~~

             * Delete as necessary

APPLICATION

~~Miss~~)
Mrs) ..SIMPSON....... Forenames Susan June......
~~Mr~~)

Date of birth .22.June.1943.....

Address ...16.Longmead.Lane.......................

..........Northfields.............................

..........MANCHESTER. MA6.5BL... Tel no 695318...

Date .3.September.19--. Signature *S.J. Simpson*

Circular letters

A company will send out circular letters when it wishes the same letter to go to a large number of people. These letters may be printed, produced on a word processor or otherwise duplicated. Sometimes these letters are formal with no personal details, and may begin 'Dear Member', 'Dear Policyholder', 'Dear Customer', etc. In others spaces may be left for the later insertion of the name and address, the name in the salutation and the date. Often, however, the date will consist of the month and year only or 'Date as postmark'. Circular letters may be signed in the usual way or left unsigned, but the typed name of the sender and designation should appear underneath, or in more formal letters may be reproduced in print.

A circular letter with spaces for personal details

```
                                        November 19--




    Dear

    I have pleasure in sending you, with our compliments,
    a copy of the TEACHER'S KEY to COMPREHENSIVE ECONOMICS
    by Shirley Jones and Peter Walters, published in
    October at £3.95.

    The key provides comprehensive answers to the com-
    plete range of questions, exercises and assignments
    contained in the main text.

    I hope you are pleased with this book.  If you would
    like to make any comments or suggestions about it,
    I would be happy to hear from you.

    Yours sincerely




    Linda Power
    Publicity Assistant



    Enc
```

Form letters

Form letters are similar to circular letters, but contain blank spaces within the body as well for variable items.

Specimen form letter

```
                                        Our Ref .......

                                        Date ..........

        Dear Customer

        Contract No: /     /        dated

        We have pleasure in confirming our acceptance of the
        contract signed by you for:

        ............ Fonansa Machine to be installed at

        .....................................................

        A photostat copy of the Contract is enclosed for
        your retention.  This Contract contains all the terms
        and conditions which have been agreed.  Please read
        it carefully.  If you think anything has been omit-
        ted you should inform us immediately.

        The sum for which the installation is to be insured
        pursuant to Clause 5 of the Contract is

        £ ..........

        Yours faithfully
        FONANSA MACHINES LIMITED




        Contracts Manager



        Enc
```

Letters and forms with tear-off slips

The line to indicate a tear-off slip may be typed with spaced or unspaced dots or hyphens, or by using the underscore. Whichever method is chosen, the line must extend from edge to edge of the paper. There should be at least one clear line space above and below the line, and preferably more if space allows.

Specimen letter with tear-off slip

SEABROOK COMMERCIAL SOCIETY

September 19--

Dear Member

The next meeting of the Society will be held on
Saturday 9 October 19-- at the Hastings Hotel,
Warren Road, Seabrook. Following lunch, the
Manager of one of the local banks will give a
talk on the effect of modern technology on the
growth of banking services.

Lunch will be served at 12.30 and will cost approximately £4.00, including potatoes, salad bar
and sweet, depending on choice. It would be
helpful if you would let me know if you wish to
have lunch by <u>Wednesday 6 October</u> so that the
Hotel can reserve table space for us.

Yours sincerely

Barry Smith
Hon Secretary

To: Mr Barry Smith, 13 Redhill Crescent, Seabrook

I hope to be present at the lunch at the Hastings
Hotel on Saturday 9 October at 12.30 pm.

Name .... Tel no ....

Address .... Guests ....

....

—————— Notice of a meeting ——————

This should be sent out well in advance to all those entitled to attend. It states the day, time, place and purpose of the meeting.

—————————— Agenda ——————————

An agenda is a list of topics to be discussed at a meeting. The topics should be arranged in local order with the routine business first. An example of a combined notice and agenda appears below.

```
THE AXON CAR CLUB

The Third Annual General Meeting of the Axon Car
Club will be held at the Royal Hotel, Broxbourne,
on Sunday 5 October 19-- at 1500 hours.

A G E N D A

1  Minutes of last meeting.

2  Treasurer's report.

3  Membership fees.

4  Election of new committee members.

5  Date of next meeting.

6  Any other business.



J Stevens
Secretary



Highbourne House
Park Street
Broxbourne, Herts.

12 September 19--
```

Chairman's agenda

In a chairman's agenda the items listed for discussion are typed down the left-hand side of the page, leaving the right-hand side blank for the chairman's notes. A left-hand margin of 25 mm (1 inch) should be allowed. A minimum of treble-line spacing should be allowed for each item. An example appears below.

Specimen layout of a Chairman's Agenda

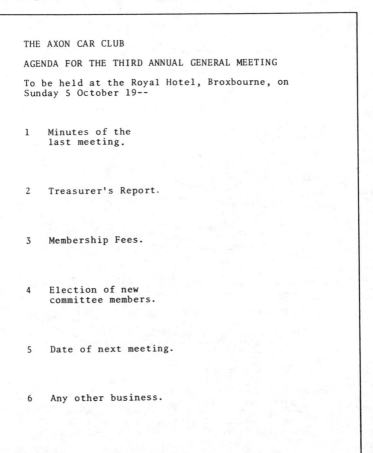

```
THE AXON CAR CLUB

AGENDA FOR THE THIRD ANNUAL GENERAL MEETING

To be held at the Royal Hotel, Broxbourne, on
Sunday 5 October 19--


1    Minutes of the
     last meeting.



2    Treasurer's Report.



3    Membership Fees.



4    Election of new
     committee members.



5    Date of next meeting.



6    Any other business.
```

Minutes

Minutes of a meeting are the official record of the proceedings of that meeting and are generally typed on A4 paper. The heading always contains the name of the club, firm or society, and the date, time and place of the meeting, and is followed by a list of those present. The items are dealt with in the order that they have been presented on the agenda. Each item is numbered and has either a shoulder heading or a marginal heading. In the example the minutes have been typed with shoulder headings.

Specimen layout for Minutes of a meeting

```
THE AXON CAR CLUB

MINUTES OF THIRD ANNUAL GENERAL MEETING

Held at the Royal Hotel, Broxbourne, on
Sunday 5 October 19-- at 1500 hours.

Present:   Mr John Price, Chairman
           Mr James Price, Vice-Chairman
           Mr P Brown
           Mr James Stevens
           Mrs P Smith
           Miss L Jackson
           Mr K R Frost
           Mr B Bacon
           Mr Alan Green, Treasurer
           Mr S P Brown, Secretary

1   NOTICE OF MEETING

    The Secretary read the notice dated 12 September
    19-- convening the meeting.

2   MINUTES OF PREVIOUS MEETING

    The Minutes of the second Annual General Meeting
    held on 3 October 19-- were read, approved and
    signed.

3   TREASURER'S REPORT

    Mr Alan Green reported that the balance of Cash in
    Hand and at the Bank was in a healthy state and
    bearing in mind the proposed outlay for a new dup-
    licator and additional stationery supplied, the
    financial position of the Club could be regarded
    as very satisfactory.
```

4   MEMBERSHIP FEES

It was unanimously decided that the membership fee
should be increased by £1.50 to £10.50.

5   ELECTION OF NEW MEMBERS

Mr Alan Brown and Miss Jill Noble were duly elected
members of the club.

6   DATE OF NEXT MEETING

The date of the next meeting was fixed for Sunday
3 December 19--.

7   ANY OTHER BUSINESS

The question of time, place and date of next
year's Rally was raised and it was decided to
postpone any decision until the next monthly
meeting.

Chairman

December 19--

Exercise 40

The following exercise is provided for extra practice in preparing and/or completing some of the real forms which you are likely to encounter in your own personal life and in the office.

1   Type a copy of the FAX form on the next page.
2   Use this form to fill in the details provided below.
3   Insert an appropriate date.
4   Make sure that you choose appropriate margins.
5   Read through the correspondence to find sender's name and address.

Send the following FAX message to:

Mr E R Bellman
Country Camping PLC
16 Northfield Street
PITLOCHRY Scotland PT7 9DG

FAX NO 08979 662301

FAX MESSAGE

<table>
<tr><td>TO</td><td>DATE</td></tr>
<tr><td>NAME</td><td></td></tr>
<tr><td>ADDRESS</td><td></td></tr>
</table>

TELEX NO
MESSAGE

FROM	DEPT

NOTE

Please arrange for two SUPRA winter weight tents, complete with all ancillary equipment, to be sent to the following address as soon as possible. We will pay cash on delivery:

B & M Altman Training Dept 3 Dean St BARNET EN9 8PY

We also require 6 TENDARTEX survival blankets, 6 sets of climbing pikes, etc so please send by FAX copies of your new brochure pages giving relevant details to us at the following number so that we can send to you an immediate order:

0810 07745967

(Add in Note) Please alert relevant department as this is an emergency situation – we have just received a commission to train a new mountain rescue team within two weeks!

13

DECIPHERING
— MANUSCRIPT – —
CORRECTION SIGNS

So far all of the copying practice has been from typewritten examples or printed matter but one of the typist's most important tasks is to decipher manuscript.

The best way of preparing to type from a handwritten original script is first to read through a fairly lengthy section. This will enable you to get to know and understand the writer's style and handwriting, and to become familiar with and understand the subject material. When there is any difficulty in understanding a word, prepare a typed draft leaving a space where the unreadable words are placed and it may well be possible subsequently to fill in the correct word when you get to know the writer's style and are conversant with the content.

Abbreviations

Whilst a comprehensive list of abbreviations is to be found on pages 201–206, some simple examples are given overleaf and these should be typed in full in the final copy of the manuscript. The first 15 are frequently used, the next 15 being more used in business and European contexts.

Abbreviation	Meaning
abt	about
aftn	afternoon
asap	as soon as possible
asst	assistant
bn	been
plse	please
sh	shall
shd	should
wk(s)	week(s)
wh	which
wd	would
wl	will
yr(s)	your(s) or year(s)
ea	each
ffy/ffly	faithfully
ETA	estimated time of arrival
ETD	estimated time of departure
EC	European Community
O/D	overdraft/overdrawn
FAO	for the attention of
HO	head office
IMF	International Monetary Fund
kg	kilogram
km	kilometre(s)
Dm	Deutschmark
fr	franc
VAT	value-added tax
AGM	annual general meeting
VDU	Visual Display Unit
P & L	Profit and Loss

Drafts are usually typed in double-line spacing, except for letters (although treble-line spacing is generally used for legal drafts as they undergo extensive revision by each party before being ready for signature).

—————— Correction signs ——————

Drafts of letters and documents contain alterations in the margins, and corrections are also made to the contents.

Generally the writer uses the following signs:

Sign in text	Sign in margin	Meaning
⅄	#	leave space
⊂		close up space
	stet ✓	*stet* (means let it stand) or a *tick* in margin but if both words are crossed out type the word with dotted line underneath
. . . .		
/		cross through word(s) or letter to be altered
⅄ ⅄	⅄ ⊙ = full stop	insert items written in margin at this point, (correction can also be put in balloon with arrow to where it is to be inserted in text)
(in our opinion)		

// or [or NP	NP	new paragraph
⌒		no new paragraph (run on)
( )	trs	transpose vertically (change over position of words or lines)
⌒ ⌒	trs	transpose horizontally (change over position of words or lines)
/ ‗	uc	change to capital letter(s)
/ ‗	lc	change from capitals to lower case

Note: Modern examining bodies use the above list when testing knowledge of proof-reading.

You will find that some instructions or alterations to drafts are contained in hand-drawn balloons and these are usually placed in the margin nearest to the word or phrase to be changed.

> 16 May recd here
> received on 30
>
> Dear Sir
> Thank you for your letter of the 30
> May. We shall be sending

Unusual or unreadable words in the text are made clearer by words (usually printed in capitals for clarity) which are placed within a dotted box in the margin.

> PREMIER
>
> It is now known that you hold the premier position in the world of athletics.

There are several variations in the form which correction signs take and particular companies may have their own individual 'house styles' when using corrections. The writer also develops his or her own particular style so the most important thing to do when typing from manuscript is to check with the person who has written the original draft to ensure that you clearly understand his or her particular marks.

Important note
The following exercises are on linked themes and contain some amendments and correction signs. They also provide the opportunity to decipher difficult handwriting. There are keys provided to each page at the end of this book to enable you to check your work.

The work on linked themes is more interesting for the person typing the correspondence. (It is now usual for NVQ examinations to take the form of correspondence and documents on linked-theme work. The typist is then able to understand the build-up of the correspondence and the resulting action that is taken by any of the parties receiving the letters, etc.)

Exercise 41

Nowadays it is possible to present information in an exciting and interesting way when giving a lecture or audio-visual presentation to an audience. The operator can use video projectors connected directly to a computer, and from there to a television screen. It can also be linked to conventional overhead projectors to show the image on screen and such methods can also be used in colleges and schools. The viewers can then see exactly what is stored on the computer being transferred to a large television screen.

Other exciting innovations are the availability of computers which are portable and work from batteries. They allow the facilities of the electronic office to be carried in a small and lightweight machine which can be used on cars, trains and aircraft whilst travelling worldwide. Afterwards, the user returns to his permanent office location and links into the computer network to integrate his new material to the system.

(Key on page 207)

Exercise 42

Today's Date

HOME ADDRESS

Westoby & Sheerwater PLC
369 Church St Gardens
EDMONTON
N9 7YT

Dear Sirs

POST AS PERSONAL ADMINISTRATOR – PERSONNEL DEPT
I am enclosing my application form for
the above post in yr Co.

ABBREVIATIONS IN FULL

Should I be fortunate enough to be ~~eventually~~
considered as a possible candidate I would be
able to attend an interview at any time to
suit you except on .... when I have
x° to attend a Glasgow Conference in on
behalf of my Company.

yet   Yours ~~faithfully~~ ~~sincerely~~

(YOUR OWN NAME)
enc

(Key on page 208)

Exercise 43

Use your own name, details and experience to complete this form after your have typed it. The position for which you are applying is Personal Assistant/Administrator in the Personnel Department. Sign and date the form.

WESTOBY & SHEERWATER PLC
369 Church St Gdns
EDMONTON   N9 7YT

(Spaced Caps)

(Centre each line)

JOB APPLICATION FORM

Title of Job................................. Dept...............

APPLICANT'S FULL NAME (BLOCK CAPITALS)

SURNAME _ _ _ _ _ _ _ _ _ _ _ FIRST NAMES _ _ _ _ _

ADDRESS _ _ _ _ _ _ _ _ _ _ _ _ _ _ _ _ _ _ _

_ _ _ _ _ _ _ _ _ _ _ _ POST CODE _ _ _ _ _

DATE OF BIRTH _ _ _ _ _ _ _ _ NATIONALITY _ _ _ _ _

EDUCATIONAL QUALIFICATIONS (Please give dates)

School _ _ _ _ _ _ _ _ _ _ _ _ _ _ _ _ _ _ _

_ _

College _ _ _ _ _ _ _ _ _ _ _ _ _ _ _ _ _ _ _

Other _ _ _ _ _ _ _ _ _ _ _ _ _ _ _ _ _ _ _

Typing Speed (if applicable) _ _ _ _ _ _ wpm

EXPERIENCE (Please give dates)

Job Title   Company Name

_ _ _ _ _ _ _ _ _ _   _ _ _ _ _ _ _ _ _

_ _ _ _ _ _ _ _ _ _   _ _ _ _ _ _ _ _ _

Salary Required _ _ _ _ _ _ _ _ _ _ _ pa

REASONS FOR APPLYING FOR THIS POST

_ _

_ _

Signed .... Date _ _ _ _ _

(Key on page 209)

Exercise 44

Jonathan Henry Miller & Sons PLC

ESTATE AGENTS
9 WEST FRONT
CAMBRIDGE CB1 8DR
Tel 0223 686 00777   FAX 0223 8634435

Our ref DM/JR/BEECH
Date

Mrs J R Finlay
Dr Rover's Cottage [H High St [Horinga] [IP32 1QR *HORRINGER*

Dr Mr Finlay

all Caps NO UNDERLINE re purchase of flat at 15 Beech Mews E9 0XLL

I am writing to ~~say~~ confirm th I have put forward ✓
yr offer of £95,600 to Miss Baine, ~~who is the~~
uc vendor. She has accepted ~~yr~~ this offer with the ✓
PROVISO proviso th, as the figure is lower than the
asking price of £105,000, she is prepared not
to include the ~~new~~ carpets, curtains + light
fittings in the sale. [Please let me know
as soon as ~~possible~~ what your views are.
Yours sincerely

DOROTHY MILLER
Manager

(Key on page 210)

TYPING

Exercise 45

Set out the following business letter with suitable spacings. Remember to type these abbreviations in full:

- & only remains in abbreviated form in address
- w = with
- max = maximum
- yr(s) = your/yours or year(s)
- Gen Man = General Manager.

(Reference)

(Today's date) *Use open punctuation (ie no commas)*

Mr J W Webb, Chief Design Engineer, Messrs John Smith & Company, 901 London Road, MAIDSTONE, MA5 6LR

Dear Mr Webb

Owing to the steady growth of our business we are moving to larger premises in Main Street, Slough, Bucks at the end of this month. The site is a particularly good one, in the heart of this industrial centre, within easy reach of London & the M4 Motorway. The transport difficulties which we have experienced in the past will now be reduced to a minimum, & early deliveries ensured. The new factory will be fully automated w a resulting increase in both the quality & quantity of our output.

We trust that you will be patient w us during this transitional period. Any delays should be minimal only & we expect to achieve max production again within five weeks.

May we take this opportunity of expressing our thanks for yr confidence in the past & we hope that the improvements we shall introduce will lead to even more business.

Yrs sinc *leave 4 clear line spaces*
J Simpson
Gen Man

— **126** —

Exercise 46

Home address

Date

The Manager
Westbury Commercial Bank PLC
uc the ~~Maltings~~
KING'S ACRE   Suffolk
IP25   6 LD

NP
Dear Sir

for overdraft   I am writing to enquire ~~your~~ whether bank world   AS
be prepared to make loan/facilities of £2,000 available
uc to me. Next month I am commencing ~~to trade~~   shet
NP
uc as a financial Services Consultant and I urgently
need to purchase a new electronic Typewriter for   lc
S/ £200 and a word processor for £800. Additionally
I shall need other small items of office equipment.
Therefore, a business ~~overdraft~~ or loan wd be ~~necess.~~   AS
essential. I have had a current, Higher Rate
several   Deposit and Tessa accounts with your bank
for / years now and, should you find it
necessary, I would be prepd to provide
appropriate security such as life ins policies.

Thank you for your help in this matter. I shd
appreciate a reply asap as the equipment is
urgently reqd.

Yours ffly

NAME IN CAPS

(Key on page 211)

Exercise 47

The standard form letter opposite is to be sent to the clients listed below. In each case the address of the property being sold is indicated. (*Note* – also on page 130 is a manuscript of the letter to Dr Avey from which, if you prefer, you can choose to work to gain extra practice in typing from manuscript.) Read the memo from Natalie Miller on page 132 to find out the price each property is being sold for; they are in order.

– *Dr Frederick Avey, 10 Birch Avenue, Church Street, Edmonton, N9 9XV*
  (selling The Thatched Cottage, Lyle Lane, Godmaston, Cambridge CB19 1BR).
– *Mr and Mrs C Huzeker, 89 South Drake Ave, Heavercreek, Ohio 45331, USA*
  (selling 75 Clay Mill lane, Claytonbury, Huntingdon PE2 9BI).
– *Ms V Stopford, 50 Holly Close, Bourne, Lincs, P10 7YG*
  (selling Winchester House, King's Mile, Cambridge C1 24IU).

Jonathan Henry Miller & Sons PLC

ESTATE AGENTS
9 WEST FRONT
CAMBRIDGE CB1 8DR
Tel 0223 686 00777   *FAX 0223 8634435*

Our ref SJ/(your own initials)

Date

addressee's name
addressee's address (no and street)
local area (if any)
town and postal code
country

Dear ... (use personalised version of salutation,
         eg Mr Mrs etc)

SALE OF .....(complete address of property to be sold)

We are pleased to advise you that we have placed an
advertisement in a local paper with a large distribution
area offering your property for sale at the agreed
price of £......... (check price from list). The
paper will be published on Friday of this week and
we anticipate a good response to our advertising.

If we receive any offers for your property, we shall
immediately contact you and take instructions
regarding the sale. It is always advisable to be
prepared to accept an offer if this falls within
your financial expectation, and we have priced your
property at a suitable figure to enable you to do this.

If we can be of any further assistance, please do
not hesitate to contact us. In the meantime we will
continue to show prospective purchasers round
your property.

Yours sincerely

Sandra Johnson
Property Consultant

Exercise 48

Jonathan Henry Miller & Sons PLC

ESTATE AGENTS
9 WEST FRONT
CAMBRIDGE CB1 8DR
Tel 0223 686 00777   *FAX 0223 8634435*

Our ref SJ/

DR FREDERIC AVEY
10 BIRCH AVENUE,
CHURCH STREET,
EDMONTON, N9 9XV

use lower case with initial caps except use caps for EDMONTON

Dear DR AVEY

SALE OF ~~10 BIRCH AVENUE, CHURCH STREET, EDMONTON N9 9XV~~ THE THATCHED COTTAGE, LYLE LANE, GODMANTON, CAMBRIDGE CB19 1BR

We are pleased to advise you that we have placed an ~~advertisement~~ photograph in a local paper with a large distribution area offering your property for sale at the agreed price of ~~£119,000~~ 159,000 (~~check price from list~~).

The paper will be published on friday of this week and we anticipate a good response to our ~~advertising~~ advertisement. std

[If we receive any offers for your

---

property, we shall immediately contact you and take instructions regarding the sale. It is always advisable to be prepared to accept an offer if this falls within your financial expectation, and we have priced your property at a suitable figure to enable you to do this.

If we can be of any further assistance, please do not hesitate to contact us. In the meantime we will continue to show prospective purchasers round your property.

Yours sincerely

SANDRA JOHNSON
PROPERTY CONSULTANT — *be with initial caps*

(Key on page 212)

Exercise 49

MEMORANDUM

TO   Sandra Johnson, Property Consultant

FROM   Natalie Miller, Executive Director

MARGIN
1¼"
APPROX

MARGIN
1" APPROX

DATE

SUBJECT ADVERTISEMENTS FOR NEW PROPERTIES

I am sending you the 3 latest advertisements which we need to publish in the

uc
NP
#1
"huntingdon and cambridge Weekly Herald" this week. //Please check ~~that~~ that all the details are ~~correct~~ price, description, etc and then notify the

lc
Clients that we are advertising (these) properties for sale as from next

uc
friday's edition. // The photographs NP are arriving from the processors

✓ ⊙ ~~today~~ *tomorrow* I think you will find that the "Herald" needs to have our advertisements (four) days before publication.

Run on
This is a new ~~expanding~~ *growing* local

trs
paper with a distribution which

h ✓   *covers a*
    Wide area around Cambridge and
    Huntingdon and we should have some
    good response to our (advert.) *IN FULL*

close up   I would appreciate any comments on
    potential improvements etc which you

tns   may wish to make as I (feel sometimes)
    that our descriptions of properties

move   could be dynamic and (appealling.) *? spelling*

INSERT A

NP   [Please let me know as soon as
    You have organised this and ~~and~~
    send me a copy of the PROOFS

---

1) Deceptively spacious thatched cottage with good sized grounds,
   situated in quiet village opposite church - 3 beds, 2 rec,
   garage, stable block and barn. £150,000. Ref QD 46.
   (GODMASTON)

2) Beautifully refurbished detached house in semi-rural position
   with large gardens, garage, 3 beds, large kitchen. £132,000.
   Ref QD 47. (CLAYTONBURY)

3) Just reduced for quick sale - 4 bed terraced Georgian house in
   city centre, 3 reception rooms, off-street parking for 3 cars,
   short distance from river (mooring rights also available)
   £140,000. Ref QD 48. (CAMBRIDGE)

(Key on page 213)

Exercise 50

THE PROPERTY LETTING CENTRE
Head Office: 24 Lynton Close Elm End Rd
/W   WATFORD WD3 7KKM

(in full) Our ref: BKCM/ht   Telephone 0923 1200099
4 Sept 199-   Fax 0923 1226565
Mr D A V Jackson
Avenida de Alvarode
Vascenceles 2993
2711 SINTRA
Portugal

Dear Mr Jackson

Re: 15 Beechwood Mews, Harewood St, Potters Bar

Further to our visit to the above flat on 31 Aug (in line) 199-, we are pleased to confirm that, as agreed, we have placed property details of the on our books at a rental charge of £520 per calendar month. As you are aware, the rental income will be inclusive of maintenance, ground rent, rate for & water which you are currently responsible. The services such as Gas, Telephone and Electricity will be payable by the Tenants and they will be informed by us to sign for the supply source of prior to their occupation.

We always advertise our properties only to Professional lc Persons and we take up their references on your behalf. A deposit of one month's rental plus £100 booking fee is paid to us plus the one month's rental in advance. We then deduct our fees from this sum and forward to you an account plus the balance of the monies due to you.

run on

uc If you require any alteration to this arrangement, ie for this company to pay the monies into an English bank account on your behalf we shall be pleased to do this for you. [It may be that you will find that you will need to make use of our lc Full Property Management Service whilst you are staying for an indefinite period abroad, and, if you should require any further information, please do not hesitate to contact this Company.

INDEFINITE

stet

run on

In the meantime I enclose our brochure containing details of the full management service we provide.

Yours Sincerely

WENDY MACPHERSON

Property Letting Manager

enc

(Key on page 214)

Exercise 51

Type a copy of this brochure to send with the letter to Mr Jackson.

(centre) THE PROPERTY LETTING CENTRE

(ALL CAPS) this brochure is to give you information regarding our two services of property letting. Both services include a free valuation of your property/to ascertain that a correct rental is to be charged.
(by our expert valuer)

(uc) The first, which is a full management service, guarantees that this company will find you a suitable professional person to rent your property for six monthly (or one yearly) periods. The Company takes up full financial and personal references on your behalf and collects the rents as and when/due. A full tenancy [these become uc] shorthold agreement is drawn up and signed by both parties. The full management service means that you have space and peace of mind as/should any repairs etc become necessary/the company (sh/work) arranges for the appropriate/to be worked carried out, and debits your a/c accordingly. This is a particularly suitable service for owners who are too busy to supervise the letterings personally or (uc) who are living abroad. /there is a charge of 12 per cent for this service.

(ALL CAPS) We offer the second service which is a part management service where this Company guarantees to find a suitable professional person to rent your property for six monthly or one yearly periods. The Company takes up full financial and personal references on y/our behalf and collects the rents as and when due. A full (uc) tenancy agreement is drawn up and signed by /both parties/This is ⊙ a suitable service for owners who are able to/supervise the letting personally and arrange their own repai/rs. There is a charge of 10 per cent for this service. Should you require to change over from the part management service to full management at any time during the tenancy/this can be arranged at a fee of two per cent extra. /period/

(s/uc ALL CAPS) in both service/the Tenant will be asked to provide a deposit of one month's rental in ad/vance and to pay his or her rent by standing order at a bank or through a building society. trs

---

(Key on page 216)

Exercise 52

Before commencing this exercise read carefully through and learn the following abbreviations. In the letter these must be typed in full.

Sep = September, ref = reference, advert = advertisement, shl = shall, wl = will, poss = possible, & = and, wrk = work, Oct = October, wd = would, St = Street, max = maximum, mnth = month, m/c = machine, htg = heating, wrkd = worked, yr = your (or year), Yrs = Yours, fthfly = faithfully.

---

24 Sep 19..

The Manager
Property Letting Centre
24B Lynton Close
Elm End Road
WATFORD   WD3 7KM

35 East Barnes Ave
Dykes Bury
MIDDLESBROUGH
Cleveland
NT3 37LK

Telephone No 0642 /224439 /87

Dear sir

[With ref to your advert in today's edition of the 'Daily provincial and Cleveland Echo'. I shl be grateful if you wl kindly send me as soon as poss details of the 2 flats you have available – ref numbers G789 and G901.   [G]

[I am commencing wrk in central london on 10 Oct and am urgently in need of a fully furnished 2 bedroom flat near to a railway station that wd be convenient for commuting to Liverpool St station.

— **137** —

The max rental I am prepared to pay is £130 per week or £550 per calendar month mnth.

[The flat must have an automatic washing m/c, tumble dryer, fridge, freezer, cooker extractor hood, r some form of central htg. I do also need good parking facilities to be available nearby, preferably on the premises.

[In order to save time I am enclosing the names and addresses of 2 referees to whom you can write and you will note that one is my employer in Middlesbrough for whom I have wrked for 5 years.

[I plan to visit london on 28 Sep and, if I like the flat after viewing it, I shl be prepared to sign a contract immediately and move in on 30 Sep or as soon after that date as is poss.

Thank you for yr help in this matter.

Yrs fthfly

Belinda Richardson (Miss)

enc

(Key on page 217)

Exercise 53

This is an example of a fully blocked letter. Use the same margins as for the previous letter (18 and 83 Elite, 10 and 75 Pica).

———— ABC TRAVEL LODGE ————
CLUBS PLC

PRINCETON HOUSE
23–30 TWINING ROAD LONDON SW2V 1QT

Telephone 041 3456 4537566   Fax 041 3456 467388

Our ref blj/rh/2349866/2/3

14 September 199-

Miss B L Cross
22 Little Heath Close
Muswell Hill
London N10 8UK

Dear Miss Cross

re HOLIDAY BOOKING NO 2349866/2/3

Thank you for your letter of 10 September regarding yours *(& Mrs Martine's)*
accommodation for the above holiday. I am pleased to confirm
that we have arranged your booking as follows: *(2 bedrooms,*
Luxury apartment with balcony, 2 en suite bathrooms, use of sauna,
swimming pool, jacuzzi (25 Oct to 10 Nov inclusive). *(Health Club,)*

[The address of
your hotel is: WAVECREST HOTEL, DEL MAR, SAN DIEGO,
CALIFORNIA, USA, *and,*

I confirm that a Holiday Club rental car (Granada) ~~has been booked~~ *is being booked*
and will be awaiting you at San Diego airport on 24 October when

#NB leave one clear line

you land at ~~12.30 pm.~~ 5.30pm.

Air tickets *and all travel documents* with Blue Sky Airways will be sent to you 10 days
before departure, together with the vouchers for the six weeks'
vacation in Del Mar.

You will also receive confirmation of your free one week car hire
and we do suggest that, should you wish to add additional weeks #/
to the car hire, you book it with us ~~now~~ as we now have a very
favourable car hire rate available as a special offer. #/
Thank you for using our travel services, and please do not
hesitate to contact us should you have any further queries.
May we wish you both a very enjoyable holiday.

Yours sincerely

Travel Director *of ABC*

NB Please leave 4 clear spaces for signature

(Key on page 219)

14

DISPLAY WORK

Display work involves the neat and orderly arrangement of the text so that the complete typewritten work will be pleasing to the eye and also easily read. The best examples of display work are to be found in printed matter – chiefly handbills, title-pages, notices, programmes, menus, etc. The printer has a wider selection of typefaces to choose from than most typewriters, but with the skilful use of lower and upper case letters, the underscore, and the variation of spacing between letters, words and lines the typist can secure emphasis in many different ways and display typewritten work attractively.

Use of space

Display work requires skill in the use of space and paper selection. It is not always necessary to centre everything, and indeed modern practice is to 'block' as much as possible in order to save time. However, there are occasions when centring will be necessary and two methods are described.

Refer back to page 17 for the number of spaces across a page of A4 and A5, and take as an example the title of this book:

TEACH YOURSELF TYPING

Insert A5 landscape paper (longer side at top) into the machine, making sure that the left-hand edge is at zero. Set the carriage position indicator at 50 for Elite (half 100), or 41 for Pica (half 82), and then backspace once for every two letters or spaces in the heading. To reach the point at which to start typing the heading, it will be necessary to backspace ten times. Odd letters should always be ignored. Where the material to be typed consists of several centred lines, move the margin stops out of the way and set the tabulator stop at the middle of the page to save time.

Another method of centring is first to count the number of letters and spaces in the heading and then subtract the total from the number of spaces in the width of the paper. For A5 landscape, using Elite type and the same title, 20 is subtracted from 100, giving a remainder of 80. This

---

ORGANISATIONS SUPPORTING THE ENTERPRISE

British Aerospace (Aircraft)

British Aerospace (Dynamics)

Cadbury Schweppes

Dickinson Robinson Group

Harveys of Bristol

Imperial Group

Mardon Packaging International

Newman Industries

Rolls Royce

---

number divided by two shows the point of the scale (40) at which the line should begin.

When the heading is to be placed over matter that has unequal margins, the matter will be arranged immediately over the width of the line of writing, not the width of the paper. If, for example, for binding purposes there is a left-hand margin of 15 and a right-hand margin of 5 (or a writing line of 80 spaces) the above book title would begin at 45 on the scale.

Vertical centring

Refer again to page 17 and it will be seen that the number of lines *down* a page of A5 landscape is 35. To display the list on page 142 vertically, count the number of lines in the list *including the line spaces*. In this case there are 20. Subtract this figure from 35 and the answer is 15. Divide 15 by two (ignore the half) and the answer is 7. From the top edge of the paper, turn down $7+1$ (8) line spaces, since the first space will be used up by a line of type.

If a piece of display contains 42 lines, for example, and A4 paper is being used, then the following calculation is necessary: $70-42\div2+1 = 15$. The typing will start on the *fifteenth* line from the top.

Borders and rules

Freak arrangements and the elaborate use of decorative effects are usually avoided in business, but borders and rules can be arranged attractively. The best effect is obtained with little or no ornamentation and extreme simplicity. The following are examples:

```
=======================================================
: : : : : : : : : : : : : : : : : : : : : : : : : : : : : : : : : : : :
=======================================================

---------------------------------------------------------

=======================================================
XXXXXXXXXXXXXXXXXXXXXXXXXXXXXXXXXXXXXXXXXXXXXXXXXX
=======================================================
```

Tail pieces

A decorative effect is sometimes desired at the end of chapters or sections, and arrangements of characters suitable for this purpose are:

```
---ooOoo---    ---:::::---    --xxXxx--
```

Display examples

The examples on pages 144–147 are representative of work that can be accomplished on the typewriter.

```
/////////////////////////////////////////

    T H E R E    I S    A    F I R E

  E V E R Y    O T H E R    M I N U T E

        You can't be too careful!


/////////////////////////////////////////
```

```
X-X-X-X-X-X-X-X-X-X-X-X-X-X-X-X-X-X-X

C O U G H S    a n d    S N E E Z E S

      S P R E A D    D I S E A S E S

Stay in your own home and keep warm
X-X-X-X-X-X-X-X-X-X-X-X-X-X-X-X-X-X-X
```

```
ooo-ooo-ooo-ooo-ooo-ooo-ooo-ooo-ooo
                ( give the exact fare
P L E A S E  (
                ( name your destination
H E L P    T H E    C O N D U C T O R
ooo-ooo-ooo-ooo-ooo-ooo-ooo-ooo-ooo
```

XXX

——— M U S I C ——

1. Overture	Life's Laughter	Rust
2. Selection	Mikado	Sullivan
3. Waltz	Bal Masque	Fletcher
4. Suite	Carmen	Bizet
5. Selection	Rose Marie	Friml
6. Intermezzo	Longing	Haydn Wood
7. Waltz	Count of Luxembourg	Lehar
8. Selection	Merrie England	German
9. Suite	The Royal Fireworks	Handel
10. Entr'acte	Lovely Night	Ganne
11. Waltz	The Song is Ended	Berlin
12. Selection	Scotch Airs	Myddleton

THE ELITE ORCHESTRA
under the direction of
MISS EILEEN NIGHTINGALE

XXXXXXXXXXXXXXXXXXXXXXXXXXXXXXXXXXXXXXXXXXXXXXXXXXXX

KNIGHTS OF THE
ROUND TABLE

FIVE PLAYS FROM THE
ARTHURIAN LEGEND

by

L. du GARDE PEACH

———oOo———

LONDON

Pitman Books Limited

In the menu that appears below, accents are indicated. These should be inserted in black ink if an accent key is not available on the keyboard.

```
::::::::::::::::::::::::::::::::::::::::::::::::::::::

                         M E N U

                         ─────────

                          Soup

                    Consommé Royale
                     Thick Oxtail

                          Fish

                   Fillets Lemon Sole
                     Tartare Sauce

                         Joints

         Braised Sweetbreads and Macédoine
             Roast Chicken and Sausage

                      Vegetables

           Spinach         New Potatoes

                        Sweets

            Trifle         Peach Melba

                        Coffee


::::::::::::::::::::::::::::::::::::::::::::::::::::::
```

In Exercise 54 (page 148) various items are given for centring practice; count the number of letters and spaces required for each item and centre each line across a sheet of A4 paper. Allow double spacing between each item, and also centre the exercise vertically. Where there is a space between the letters in a word, leave *three* spaces between the words.

Exercise 54

Centre the following headings, first using closed capitals, then in spaced capitals. You will find that you may need to use more than one line for the longer headings when using spaced caps, and in this case each line has to be separately calculated.

POST OFFICE GUIDE
BALANCE SHEET AND PROFIT AND LOSS ACCOUNT
INFORMATION TECHNOLOGY
HEALTH AND SAFETY LAWS
THE SECOND RUSSIAN REVOLUTION
THE UNITED STATES OF AMERICA
TEACH YOURSELF BOOKS
HER MAJESTY'S STATIONERY OFFICE
BRITISH RAIL
THE TIMES
DAILY EXPRESS
DAILY MAIL
ABC TRAVEL LODGE CLUBS PLC
BARCHAM'S BANK PLC
THE PROPERTY LETTING CENTRE
SECRETARIAL DUTIES TODAY
COMMERCIAL TYPEWRITING
ANTIQUE AND COLLECTORS' FAIR
EUROPEAN CENTENARY CLOTHING AND FASHION EXHIBITION
OLYMPIC SPORTSWEAR COLLECTION
MYTHS OF THE MEDITERRANEAN

Exercise 55

Type the following, displaying attractively across the page.
Set a tab at 35 spaces in from the left-hand margin.

LIST OF USEFUL PHRASES WHEN VISITING FRANCE
Words not easily translated without a special dictionary

HOW TO ADDRESS PEOPLE YOU MEET

this is very good	c'est très bon
that is very kind of you	c'est très gentil de votre part
may I introduce you	permettez-moi de vous présenter
to (some friends)	(quelques amis)
help yourself	servez-vous
are you on holiday	est-ce que vous êtes en vacances
do you like France	est-ce que vous aimez la France
may I use your telephone	puis-je utiliser votre téléphone

I wish to change some francs	Je voudrais changer des francs
what is the rate of exchange today	quel est le cours du change aujourd'hui
can I cash	puis-je encaisser . . . .
please	s'il vous plaît

USEFUL PLACES IN A TOWN, ETC

hotel	le pension/l'hôtel	bathroom = la salle de bain	
post office	le bureau du poste	bath = le bain	
bank	la banque	room = la chambre	
shop	le magasin	mail = les lettres, le courrier	
restaurant	le restaurant	train = le train	

USEFUL ARTICLES TO PURCHASE, AND ESSENTIAL WORDS TO KNOW

dictionary = le dictionnaire	help = une assistance
postcard = la carte postale	friend = un ami
stamp = le timbre	girl = une fille
pen = le stylo	woman = une femme
paper = le papier	boy = un garçon
newspaper = le journal	man = un homme
guidebook = le guide	town = une ville
soap = le savon	taxi = un taxi
toothbrush = la brosse à dents	road map = une carte routière
toothpaste = le dentifrice	bus = l'autobus
deodorant = le dédorant	church = l'église
suntan lotion = le lait solaire	supermarket = un supermarché

FOODS AND DRINK

roll = le petit pain	plaice = la plie
butter = le beurre	pear = la poire
coffee = le café	frozen = le surgelé
tea = le thé	meat = la viande
wine = le vin	sugar = le sucre
eggs = les oeufs	milk = le lait
fish = le poisson	ice cream = la glace
veal = le veau	drinking water = une eau potable

15

TABULAR WORK ___ AND ACCOUNTS

The work in this section is really an extension of the previous instructions regarding the display and the centring of typewritten matter, and deals with the orderly arrangement of columns across a page. Careful planning is required for good results.

The devices used for tabular work vary on different machines, but generally pressing a key or bar moves the carriage to the position at which stops have been set.

—— Estimating width and depth ——

Examine the matter to be typed carefully in order to gauge the maximum width and depth required for the complete work. Count the number of characters or characters and spaces in the widest line of each column or heading. An equal number of spaces should be left between each column (three, four or five are best) and these should be included. Subtract the combined total from the number of spaces in the width of the paper (page 17) and divide by two. This is the point at which the left-hand margin stop should be set. Tap the space bar once for each character in the widest line of the first column and for the spaces following, and set a tab stop for the second column. Repeat the procedure until tab stops have been set for all the columns. Both margins will then be equal. On occasion, of course, this tabular work may be placed on a page with ordinary text either starting at the left-hand margin or centred and will not form a distinct item.

———— Tabular examples ————

An estimate of the space required for the following example will show how to plan a tab.

FEBRUARY

Sunday	1	8	15	22
Monday	2	9	16	23
Tuesday	3	10	17	24
Wednesday	4	11	18	25
Thursday	5	12	19	26
Friday	6	13	20	27
Saturday	7	14	21	28

If five spaces are allowed between the columns, the total number of spaces required for the table is 36. For A5 landscape with Elite type, subtract 36 from 100 and divide by two. The answer, 32, is the point for the left-hand margin. Tap the number of letters in the longest word, Wednesday, plus 5 for the following space and set the first tab stop. Tap one for the second column plus 5 and set the tab stop for the second column. Continue until all the stops have been set.

To centre the table vertically, count the number of lines in the table (16), subtract from 35, divide by two (ignore the fraction) and add one. The typing should start on the *tenth* line down from the top.

Type this example in double spacing on A5 paper and then try Exercises 56 and 57 in the same manner.

Note that although main headings may be centred if desired, it is easier and quicker to block them at the left hand margin as shown.

Exercise 56

PRESENTS OF THE UNITED STATES 1923–1981

1	Calvin Coolidge	Rep.	1923–9
2	Herbert C Hoover	Rep.	1929–33
3	Franklin D Roosevelt	Dem.	1933–45
4	Harry S Truman	Dem.	1945–53
5	Dwight D Eisenhower	Rep.	1953–61
6	John F Kennedy	Dem.	1961–3
7	Lyndon B Johnson	Dem.	1963–69
8	Richard M Nixon	Rep.	1969–74
9	Gerald R Ford	Rep.	1974–76
10	James Carter	Dem.	1976–81

Table with column headings

Column headings are best typed at the tab stop positions and are regarded as part of the column when making calculations. Leave a clear line space after the heading.

Type the example in double spacing on A5 landscape paper, making the necessary calculations, and then try Exercises 58 and 59 on the same size paper. Exercise 58 may be typed in double spacing, but Exercise 59 should be typed in single spacing. It is suggested that the Arabic and Roman numerals be lined up *to the left*, so that each numeral begins at the same point, blocked under the heading.

Exercise 57

List of Subjects

Accountancy	Dietetics	Mathematics	Printing
Advertising	Economics	Metallurgy	Refrigeration
Aeronautics	Elocution	Mineralogy	Salesmanship
Architecture	Engineering	Mining	Shipping
Arithmetic	English	Music	Shorthand
Banking	First Aid	Needlework	Sociology
Book-keeping	Geography	Optics	Telecommunications
Bridging	History	Pharmacy	Television
Calculation	Insurance	Photography	Theatre
Chemistry	Investment	Physics	Transport
Commerce	Journalism	Poetry	Typewriting

(Key on page 221)

Example of a table with column headings

LOCAL GOVERNMENT – DIVISION OF FUNCTIONS

Service	Metropolitan areas	Non-Metropolitan areas	Greater London
Education	District	County	Borough
Personal social services	District	County	Borough
Police and fire services	County	County	GLC
Planning	Shared	Shared	Shared
Highways	Shared	Shared	Shared
Environmental Health	District	District	Borough
Housing	District	District	Borough

Exercise 58

The Grand National

Year	Horse	Jockey	Owner
1972	Well to Do	G Thorner	Capt. T Forster
1973	Red Rum	B Fletcher	Mr N le Mare
1974	Red Rum	B Fletcher	Mr N le Mare
1975	L'Escargot	T Carberry	Mr R Guest
1976	Rag Trade	J Burke	Mr P Raymond
1977	Red Rum	T Stack	Mr N le Mare
1978	Lucius	B R Davies	Mrs D Whitaker
1979	Rubstic	M Barnes	Mr J Douglas
1980	Ben Nevis	C Fenwick	Mr R Stewart Jnr
1981	Aldaniti	R Champion	Mrs V Embericos

(Key on page 222)

Exercise 59

Arabic and Roman Numerals

Arabic	Roman small	Roman Capitals	Arabic	Roman small	Roman Capitals
1	i	I	15	xv	XV
2	ii	II	16	xvi	XVI
3	iii	III	17	xvii	XVII
4	iv	IV	18	xviii	XVIII
5	v	V	19	xix	XIX
6	vi	VI	20	xx	XX
7	vii	VII	30	xxx	XXX
8	viii	VIII	40	xl	XL
9	ix	IX	50	l	L
10	x	X	60	lx	LX
11	xi	XI	70	lxx	LXX
12	xii	XII	80	lxxx	LXXX
13	xiii	XIII	90	xc	XC
14	xiv	XIV	100	c	C

(Key on page 223)

Ruling in ink

Tabular work may be ruled either with the underscore or in ink. In the latter instance, a black ballpoint pen is best. Guide dots (light impressions of the full stop) may be inserted to ensure accuracy. These should be centred between each section to be ruled. The dots for the outside vertical lines should be placed at a point equal to half the number of spaces between the columns. The ruling, which will obscure the guide dots, will be inserted after the paper has been removed from the typewriter. Alternatively, guide dots may be indicated and ruled lines drawn lightly in pencil after the paper has been removed from the machine. Enclose the table first by measuring 5 mm from the typing on all four sides, then with the help of carefully-measured guide dots draw in the remaining vertical and horizontal lines. All traces of pencil markings should be erased after the lines have been inked over. Allow a clear line space above and below horizontal rulings within the table. Column headings in ruled tables should not be underscored and should be in single line spacing.

When there are varying widths of line in a column it is advisable to insert leader dots to link up related items in other columns. These leader dots are best typed in a continuous line, as shown on page 107.

Copy the examples which follow and then type Exercise 60 in single spacing on A5 paper, using the blocked style.

Example of a ruled tab in the blocked style

N E W   B O N D   I S S U E S

INCOME FOR EACH £1000 INVESTED

Age at Commencement	Income received annually	Equivalent Gross Yield to Basic Taxpayer
	£	%
25	73.31	9.37
35	73.43	9.38
45	73.50	9.50
55	74.30	9.60

The same tab fully centred

N E W   B O N D   I S S U E S

INCOME FOR EACH £1000 INVESTED

Age at Commencement	Income received annually	Equivalent Gross Yield to Basic Taxpayer
	£	%
25	73.31	9.37
35	73.43	9.38
45	73.50	9.50
55	74.30	9.60

Exercise 60

THE PRINCIPAL NATIONAL DAILIES

Paper	Proprietors	Circulation in 19-- (millions)
Daily Express	Trafalgar House	2.4
Sun	News International	3.8
Daily Mail	Associated Newspapers	1.9
Daily Mirror	Reed Publishing Holdings	3.6
Daily Star	Trafalgar House	0.9
Daily Telegraph	Daily Telegraph	1.3
Financial Times	Pearson Longman	0.8
Guardian	Guardian and Manchester	0.4
	Evening News	
Morning Star	Morning Star Co-op Society	0.03
The Times	News International	0.3

(Key on page 224)

Typing figures in column form for calculation

Care should be taken to see that units are under units, tens under tens, etc, and that the decimal points are lined up underneath one another. When the blocked style is being used, the currency sign above columns of money should be placed over the first digit. Otherwise it may be placed over the decimal point or over the units column of pounds.

The £ in the total should be typed close up to the figures, and the lines above and below the total should not extend beyond the figures. Use the variable line spacer for the lower total line.

The following examples illustrate the recommended spacing above and below totals:

1 *Single* *spacing*	**2** *1½-line* *spacing*	**3** *Double* *spacing*
£	£	£
396.24	396.24	396.24
364.00	364.00	364.00
25.53	25.53	25.53
15.38	15.38	15.38
£801.15	£801.15	£801.15

Turn up ½ (1)
Turn up 1½ (2)
Turn up ½ (2)

Turn up 1 (3)
Turn up 2 (3)
Turn up 1 (3)

Practise these examples and then type Exercise 61 in single spacing on A5 paper, using the blocked style of layout.

Exercise 61

Electra Machine
Quarterly Sales

Branch	March	June	Sept	Dec
Southampton	136	210	195	187
Portsmouth	125	167	154	170
Liverpool	103	141	139	126
Birmingham	214	230	179	223
Manchester	212	176	194	182
Leeds	317	265	276	284
Sheffield	284	314	237	330
Burnley	147	201	169	229
Middlesbrough	231	198	217	186
Cardiff	246	312	256	306
Swansea	193	224	184	219
Newport	231	189	209	196
Totals	2,439	2,627	2,409	2,638

(Key on page 225)

Accounts

These are usually typed on A4 paper – either on single sheets or on two separate sheets which are joined together when the work is complete. The columns in the account should be separated, if possible, by three character spaces. Calculation for spacing and margins should be made as for tabulation.

The longer side should be typed first so as to determine the line on which the totals should appear. The shorter side will be typed to correspond. A suggested layout for a receipts and payments account, which is the type of account most used by clubs and charitable societies, appears on the next page.

Specimen layout of a Receipts and Payments Account

```
                        AXON CAR CLUB

                Receipts and Payments Account

                for the year ended 30 April 19--

        £         £                          £           £

Balance at Bank    2053.10   Bulletin:
Subscriptions       125.00     Stationery    243.80
Car Badges           38.70     Postage       192.60
                               Duplicating   125.00     561.40
Bank Interest         5.70
                             Telephone                    36.75

                             AGM 19--                     64.00

                             Xmas Party                  110.00

                             Car Badges                  225.00

                             Bank Charges                 22.00

                             Balance at Bank            1203.35

                  £2222.50                             £2222.50
```

16
TECHNICAL, LEGAL AND LITERARY WORK

Mathematical and scientific expressions

Although special keyboards can be obtained for technical work, it is often necessary for the typist to use a standard keyboard. This work may involve typing mathematical expressions or chemical formulae containing superior or inferior characters (ie characters above or below the normal writing line), and writing in some symbols by hand.

Allow a space above and below the expressions when they form part of continuous prose and a space either side of mathematical signs within the expression. Unless a special typewriter is available, the interliner or half-line spacing must be used for the superior and inferior characters. Where there are several of these in a line it is quicker to leave spaces for them, filling them in after the other characters have been typed. Within an expression, characters on one line should be centred between those on two.

Practise the following:

$2x + 3y = 12$

$(x - 7)(x - 2) = x^2 - 9x + 14$

% gain in price $= \dfrac{(6 - 5)}{5} \times 100\% = 20\%$

$2NaHCO_3 - CaCl_2 + 2H_2O + 2NH_3$

$y = \sqrt{2x - 1}$ $\qquad\qquad$ Area $= \pi R^2 - \pi r^2$

Legal work

Specifications

A specification contains particulars of work to be carried out. A4 paper is generally used, and the subheadings may be typed in the margin for quick reference. Double- or single-line spacing is permissible, according to the length. The example on pages 170–171 shows one method of layout. As with most documents, there are variations of style and employers' preferences should always be followed.

Wills

A will is a document providing for the distribution or administration of property after the death of the testator. Special parchment is used and the document is typed in double-line spacing. The opening words and the first words of each clause are typed in capitals, as shown in the specimen overleaf. The left-hand margin may be set at 24 for Elite type (20 for Pica type) and the attestation clause at 18 for Elite type (15 for Pica type), so as to ensure that there is ample space for the signature of the testator and the witnesses. A4 paper may be used for practice.

Codicils

A simple alteration to a will as it stands can be done by making a codicil. This is nothing more than a supplement to a will. The codicil is typed in similar style to the will as shown in the specimen on page 169.

Endorsements

The endorsement is typed on the back of the document and should contain the date, the names of the parties, a brief description of the contents and sometimes the name of the solicitors by whom the document has been prepared.

Special parchment is used for this document, which can be folded into four, or lengthwise into two. When folding into four, place the paper face upwards and fold it into two by placing the bottom edge level with the top edge and creasing flat; then place the folded edge with the open edges and crease again. The endorsement should be on the uppermost side when folded. For a lengthwise fold, place the paper face upwards and fold the left edge over the right edge until the two edges meet, and then crease. The endorsement should be to the right of the crease on the last sheet.

An example of an endorsement for a will is given on page 174.

Specimen layout of a will

THIS IS THE LAST WILL AND TESTAMENT of me
ALBERT BETHELL of 56 Garner Road Saint Albans
in the County of Hertford Civil Servant

1   I DIRECT the payment of all my just debts
funeral and testamentary expenses by my Executors
hereinafter named

2   I APPOINT my Wife ALICE BETHELL to be
executor and trustee of this my Will

3   I GIVE all my personal chattels unto my
wife the said Alice Bethell

4   I GIVE AND BEQUEATH unto my Brother
THOMAS BETHELL the sum of ONE THOUSAND POUNDS
if he shall be living at my death

5   I GIVE DEVISE AND BEQUEATH all my real and
personal estate whatsoever and wheresoever not
hereby or by any Codicil hereto otherwise
specifically disposed of and of which I can
dispose by Will in any manner I think proper
unto my wife the said Alice Bethell for her own
use and benefit absolutely

6   I REVOKE all former Wills and testamentary

dispositions heretofor made by me

I N   W I T N E S S   whereof I have hereunto

set my hand to this my Will this

day of

One thousand nine hundred and

SIGNED by ALBERT BETHELL the Testator)
in the presence of us both present at)
the same time who in his presence and)
in the presence of each other have   )
hereunto subscribed our names as   )
witnesses   )

Specimen layout of a codicil

THIS IS THE FIRST CODICIL TO THE WILL dated

the   day of

One thousand nine hundred and   of me

ALBERT BETHELL of 56 Garner Road Saint Albans

in the County of Hertford Civil Servant

1   I REVOKE the bequest of ONE THOUSAND POUNDS

to my Brother THOMAS BETHELL

2   I GIVE AND BEQUEATH unto my Cousin JACK FROST

of The Four Winds Breeze Lane Saint Albans

aforesaid the sum of ONE THOUSAND POUNDS

3   IN ALL OTHER RESPECTS I confirm my said Will

I N   W I T N E S S   whereof I have hereunto set

my hand to this my first Codicil this

day of

One thousand nine hundred and

SIGNED by ALBERT BETHELL the Testator)
in the presence of us both present at)
the same time who in his presence and)
in the presence of each other have   )
hereunto subscribed our names as   )
witnesses   )

Specimen layout of a specification

S P E C I F I C A T I O N of work required to be
done in the erection of a dwelling house at Epping
for Mr Frank Jones, in accordance with Drawings
prepared by Mr John Dean of 10 High Road, Epping,
the architect referred to in this specification.

10 May 19--

PRELIMINARY and GENERAL

NOTICES AND FEES
Give all requisite notices to the Local and other
Authorities, obtain all licences, and pay all fees.

SETTING-OUT
The Contractor is to set out the whole of the works in
accordance with the plans; and he will be responsible
for the correctness of the setting-out, and is to amend
the same if it shall be found by the Architect to be
incorrect.

DIMENSIONS ON
DRAWINGS

Figured dimensions are, in all cases, to be taken in preference to scale, and the large scale details to be followed in preference to small scale general drawings. In the event of any apparent discrepancy between the drawings or between the drawings and this specification, the Contractor is to ask for an explanation from the Architect before proceeding.

SCAFFOLDING

The Contractor is to supply all scaffolding and plant required for the works.

WATER AND
LIGHTING

Pay all charges for water and lighting required during the erection of the building.

Specimen layout of a section of a play

S I R   L A U N C E L O T

O F   T H E   L A K E

———oOo———

CHARACTERS

Sir Caradoc   Servant
Sir Launcelot   Merlin
Queen Morgan le Fay

A room in SIR CARADOC'S castle with a very heavy-looking door. There is no window.

At a table with fruit, wine, etc., QUEEN MORGAN LE FAY is sitting with SIR CARADOC. A SERVANT pours wine for them.

CARADOC   Leave us!

(The SERVANT goes out.)

Now you may speak freely.

MORGAN   I will. You, Sir Caradoc, have no love for Arthur, my
          brother.

CARADOC   I have no more love for him than you.

MORGAN   I hate him! But for him — and Merlin, with his magic
          arts — my husband, King Lot, would have been overlord of
          Britain. Instead of which he has to do homage to him — to
          Arthur!

CARADOC   True.

MORGAN   It is time that Arthur, with his Round Table of knights,
          was exterminated as one stamps out a nest of scorpions.

CARADOC   I should be happy to see it.

MORGAN   You shall be happy.

CARADOC   Arthur is strong, the strongest king in Britain. All
          others are lesser and tributary to him.

MORGAN   Arthur is stronger than any single king, but not stronger
          than all. Together, they could overwhelm him and his knights.

Specimen layout for an endorsement

```
                    Dated 11 January 19--




                    T H E    W I L L    OF

                 ALBERT BETHELL ESQUIRE




                 Joseph Johncock & Sons
                       Solicitors
                   15 Chipstead Road
                   COULSDON Surrey
                       CR3 3JD
```

Literature

Dramatic work

This will contain title-page, synopsis of acts and scenery, cast and characters, followed by the spoken parts. A4 paper is used.

Names of speakers are placed alongside their respective parts. All descriptive words not spoken are underlined and typed in single-line spacing. Double-line spacing is used for the dialogue. The example on pages 172–173 is from a short play by L. du Garde Peach, and the title-page of the book from which it is taken was used for the display on page 146. The extract has been typed in traditional style.

Poetry

Single poems should be typed on A4 or A5 paper according to their length, and centrally placed on the page. Single spacing should be used for the verses with two or three clear line spaces between each verse. The title is usually typed in capitals and centred over the writing line.

If successive lines rhyme or there is no rhyme at all, all the lines begin at the margin.

```
            THE LITTLE DOG'S DAY

All in the town were still asleep,
When the sun came up with a shout and a leap.
In the lonely streets unseen by man,
A little dog danced.  And the day began.
```

If, however, alternate or certain lines rhyme, or a line is very short, then these may be indented.

```
              SUSPIRA

O would I were where I would be!
   There would I be where I am not:
For where I am I would not be,
   And where I would be I can not.

                              Anon
```

A third form of displaying poetry is to centre each line, using a capital letter to start every line.

DOES A SPIDER?

Does a spider, when it dies, cry and cry
and cry for all that's lost,
Or does it wrinkle up its compound eyes,
And chuckle over captured flies,
And frightened children?

Does a spider reminisce on eaten lovers
And a stolen kiss,
Or rather does it miss
The crunching legs of cold,
dismembered insects?

Does a spider, on a spiral thread,
have spiral dreams?
Or does it dread such terrifying things,
As spiteful beaks,
And angry, pounding wings?

Does a spider in the bath, try and try
and try
To get away,
Or rather does it play a fun-packed game
Of out the window,
And up the outside drain?

Gavin S P Miller

17

PRACTICE SAMPLE LAYOUTS

All the exercises in this chapter have been designed to offer additional typing practice with an emphasis on layout.

Exercise 62

Type the following exercise on A5 portrait paper, centring horizontally and vertically.

```
            WE ARE ORGANISING A DAY TRIP TO FRANCE

                     If you are interested

                          contact

                  PERSONNEL DEPARTMENT

        Members of staff will have a 50% discount
          and can bring one guest at full price


        Travel will be by coach from the Company
          car park on Saturday 12 June at 6 am
           and return at approximately midnight

               NUMBERS ARE LIMITED
               RESERVE YOUR SEATS NOW
```

Exercise 63

Type the following exercise on A5 landscape, centring horizontally and vertically.

J U M B L E   S A L E

to be held on
SATURDAY 14 NOVEMBER
10 am to 1 pm

at

THE PRIORY HALL
GRANGE ROAD
EDMONTON N9

REFRESHMENTS AVAILABLE   CAR PARKING FACILITIES

Admission: 20p Adults
             10p Pensioners/children

Exercise 64

Type the following exercise on A5 portrait, centring horizontally and vertically.

WOULD YOU LIKE A FREE HAIRDO?

IF SO CONTACT:

The Hairdressing Department
Tristan College
92 Duncan Road
Enfield

tel: 081 732 9987
and speak to Jennifer

You will only be charged for
the materials that are used!

Exercise 65

Type the following exercise on A4 paper centring horizontally and vertically.

COMPUTER COURSES

AT A PRICE YOU CAN AFFORD

in the following subjects

WORDPROCESSING (WORDPERFECT 5.1)

DATABASE III

SPREADSHEETS (LOTUS 1 2 3)

commencing

SEPTEMBER

Details from: The Training Manager
                 Adult Training Unit
                 Elma Park Centre
                 London EN2 OJT

Telephone: 081 356 08897 or call into the Unit
                 between 9 - 4

Exercise 66

Display this itinerary on A4 portrait.

ITINERARY

Trip of Miss Janet Jones to Valencia
6 - 8 June inclusive

<u>Tuesday 6 June</u>

1430 hours	Company car from office to airport
1540	Arrive London Heathrow, Terminal 2
1645	Depart Flight 1B 615 for Valencia
2005	Arrive Valencia (1 hour ahead)
	Taxi to Hotel La Touriste

<u>Wednesday 7 June</u>

0800	Breakfast meeting with Snr Fernandez
0930	Car collect to take to Lladro
1000	Meeting with Julian Madrez
	Tour of Warehouses
1530	Return to hotel
1700	Meeting with Pedro Sulmena
2000	Dinner booked for self and 5 guests
	(Caverna, Jardines del Real - pasta
	and seafood a speciality)

<u>Thursday 8 June</u>

1030	Meeting at Musica Provincial (Snr
	Pedro Merrar)
	Suggest lunch at Bistro next door
1535	Depart Valencia Flight IB 614
	(Check in 1 hour before take off)
1655	Arrive London Heathrow, terminal 2
	Company car will collect

Exercise 67

Display the whole of this form and also complete *Section B* with Miss B L Cross's details.

Variation form

Section A

VARIATION IN MORTGAGE PAYMENT   GREAT BARTON BUILDING SOCIETY

Please read through the following and complete the
tear-off strip below if all the details given in
Section A here are still correct: THE MORTGAGE
INTEREST RATE HAS BEEN CHANGED TO 10.25% EFFECTIVE
FROM 1 DECEMBER 199-
THE REVISED PAYMENT IN THIS NOTICE SUPERSEDED ALL
PREVIOUS NOTIFICATIONS FROM THIS BUILDING SOCIETY

Account No 94-777-197-24159

Name and Address
Miss B L Cross
22 Little Heath Close
Muswell Hill
LONDON   N1O OLJ

Commencing on the date above your monthly payments will be

NET OF BASIC RATE TAX @ 25.00%   £665.38

Administration Centre, Hill Walk, BURY ST EDMUNDS   BE1 9KN

Form Number DP 4OO 3/95 JKL

Detach here and please then send this form to your
Bank to amend your old standing order

Section B

Mortgage Account No

TO ....BANK (BRANCH TITLE)

Commencing on .... please pay monthly
until this order is cancelled in writing to
British Commerce and Foreign Bank - Sorting Code
777-OO-565 for the Credit of GREAT BARTON BUILDING SOCIETY
the sum of £665.38   A/C No 94-777-197-24159

Date .... Signature...............................

Address...

Bank Account No /.../.../.../.../.../.../.../.../.../

18

SPEED
TESTS

Introduction

It may not be within the capacity of every typist to attain a championship rate, but regular practice on the exercises in the earlier sections should have secured a fair speed of operation. High speed will not be attained unless the touch system has been mastered; the eyes must be kept on the copy throughout the test.

Repetition practice

One of the most helpful methods for increasing speed is repetition on straightforward printed matter, which should be typed and retyped several times. The matter selected should be varied, and suitable pieces can be obtained from any book, magazine or newspaper; small print, however, should be avoided. The repetition practice should be abandoned immediately there is any question of partial memorisation and a new piece should then be selected.

'Strokes' and words

When the question of typewriting skill is being discussed it is usually in terms of ability to type at so many words a minute, but it is not generally understood that the word, in this context, is a measured unit. It would not be reasonable for two lengthy words to have the same time value as two short words. Take, for example, 'terminological inexactitude' for 'an untruth'. In the first rendering there are twenty-seven strokes or depressions of keys, including the space bar, and in the second there are only ten strokes or depressions.

The usual method of counting is to use an average of *five* strokes for each word. Each time a key is depressed, whether it is a character key, punctuation or the space bar, it counts as one stroke.

———— Speed test practice ————

1   Obtain an electronic timer such as a clock or watch with alarm facility, or an electric timer from a hardware store. This is needed to set a time, say three minutes to begin with, then progressing to five minutes as your speed and accuracy develops. Finally, a ten-minute test will enable you to judge your increasing speed, accuracy and endurance!

2   Practise the speed tests on the following pages by sorting out the difficult words, typing these until you feel confident and can type them at some speed. Next, decide if any difficulty has been experienced with the typing of certain phrases. After practising these to build up speed, you are then ready to try the speed test itself.

3   Use A4-size paper. Never erase any mistakes as this is a waste of time. You can, if you wish, use double-line spacing for up to 40 words per minute. Set the timer for the time span you decide upon, say three minutes to begin with, then commence typing immediately you have set the timer.

4   Stop typing when you hear the buzzer.

5 Calculate your speed as follows, using the specially counted speed tests on the following pages: Add the total number of *strokes achieved* (you will find a running total at the end of each line) and then *divide this total by five* to obtain the number of words typed in three minutes. Then *divide the total number of words by three* and you will see how fast you can type in words per minute (wpm).

Example – 600 strokes typed in three mns
   600 divided by five to obtain number of words
   = 120 words typed in three mns
   = 120 divided by three = **40 wpm**

6 Calculate whether your number of errors is within an acceptable limit (see below) and you will find that your achievements are well worth all the effort expended.

Calculation of errors

Option 1 – maximum allowance of one error for every 50 words typed (so in the above example, allow two errors for the 120 words).

Option 2 – six-error allowance is made for a five minute speed test (speed is calculated on words typed up to the seventh error)

Option 3 – one-error allowed for percentage of words, ie two or three per 100.

Types of error include: irregular line spacing; lines far too long into the right-hand margin, or too short; paragraphs haphazardly indented (indents are rarely used now); faulty line spacing down page (especially at paragraphs); faulty spacing after punctuation marks; transposed words or letters; words omitted or inserted; lines omitted; 'piling' of letters (manual machines only); irregular left-hand margins; use of erasure devices; overtyping (manuals); misspellings, etc.

Remember that, when attempting the tests, speed without accuracy is valueless. It is far better to have good quality then indifferent quantity, and an excellent motto to keep continually in mind is to 'make haste slowly'.

Exercise 68

Do not type the numbers in the right-hand column

```
The latest invention to bring pleasure to those using it is the      64
videophone.  This is a telephone with a small video screen          122
attached which works through the telephone network.  It is          181
necessary for the person at each end of the call to have            238
a similar machine and then the system can work.  The colour         298
pictures and voices are sent into a datastream which connects       360
through the normal telephone lines and there is no extra charge     424
for calls made in this way.  Now deaf people find that they can     488
use these machines to lip read the messages and, of course,         548
those with relatives living far away find the videophone most       610
comforting since they can see and talk to their family or friends.  676
There is also a button to press should you require total visible    741
privacy from the caller, or if you are seated in the bath!          800
```

(160 words)

Exercise 69

If you are using a word processor to write articles, business   62
letters or memoranda, it is very useful to explore or to consider   128
what possibilities there are available to you within the computer's   196
programs. Some authors need the facility of a prepared set of   260
margins, tab stops, etc and when this is provided it is called a   325
template. It is especially useful for long reports or extended   390
documents to be printed on A4 paper or continuous stationery.   452
For this type of work a special set of templates is provided   513
from which a choice can be made. Each template has different   575
settings to suit individual needs. Usually the pages are numbered   642
at the bottom with a page number provided on the right-hand margin   709
at the end of each page. This is particularly useful for   766
documents and numbered pages of reports.   806

(161 words)

Exercise 70

Portable language translators are an innovation which enables the 65
user to carry and use the equivalent of a large number of 123
dictionaries. They operate with a visible word display and all 187
that the user needs to do is to key in which language he wishes 251
his word or phrase to be translated into. Up to six European 312
languages can be combined in one translator which is small enough 378
to be carried in a pocket or handbag. However, no help is given 443
with an audio input so that the person using the translator does 509
not know how to pronounce the words. A language laboratory, 570
however, provides input of both written and aural information thus 637
giving the fullest experience of the new skill. It is considered 703
to be one of the most effective ways of learning a foreign 762
language with a correct pronunciation. 800

(160 words)

Exercise 71

It is a very useful fact that the house buyer can obtain tax   61
relief on interest paid to buy his or her own home. The limit   123
of the amount of relief an individual can obtain is announced   184
in the Budget each year. If the loan from a building society   245
or bank is in two names the limit of the allowance is divided   306
equally between the two people concerned, provided each name   366
appears on the title deeds of the property. So each person   425
can receive tax relief on payments of interest made.   477
It is also possible for people to choose to share jointly both   539
the limit allowed and the tax relief given in any proportion   599
they wish. For example, a wife can have all the tax relief   658
even though the loan is in her husband's name. This choice is   720
called an 'allocation of interest' election and the Inland   778
Revenue will accept a decision, provided it is made by both   837
people concerned, to share the tax relief in any proportion   896
required.   905

(181 words)

Exercise 72

It is now easy to arrange and to prepare standard letters
on word processors which store texts on disc. Any list of
names and addresses can be stored in the machine's memory
files. Then a technique known as 'mail merge' is used to
prepare data to circularise a particular letter to the names
and addresses listed. The computer can personalise each
addressee's details, eg Miss S Johnson, 6 Hill Street,
SLEAFORD. It also amends the salutation in each instance
to correspond, ie ' Dear Miss Johnson'. It can also
change the contents of the letter to correspond with the
individual's details using phrases like 'the Johnson
family has been chosen to receive' included in the body of
the letter. In this way the recipient feels that he or
she is receiving a letter meant for him or her alone.
The names and addresses can be transferred from any list
of mailing addresses to other files for the corresponding
address labels to be swiftly produced. Word processors
are not suitable for printing data on envelopes.

	58
	116
	174
	233
	294
	351
	406
	464
	517
	574
	629
	688
	744
	798
	855
	913
	969
	1018

(203 words)

Among the many other facilities provided by computers is
the ability to prepare business forms, invoices, statements,
orders, etc. Computers can also make calculations of gross
total prices, value-added tax, discounts, and net prices.
The many computerised procedures available today include
telephone directories, electronic mail, networks and file
sharing. It has also recently been made possible to give 24-
hour warnings of impending floods and other disasters by the
information calculated on computers owned by some insurance
companies; and these companies are now able to supply their
clients with notification in time for evasive action to be
taken. Doctors and surgeons increasingly use computers
for the storage and retrieval of information about patients,
about various symptons of illnesses and the many different
methods of treatment available.

57
117
176
233
289
346
406
466
525
585
643
698
758
816
849

(170 words)

Exercise 73

A new and convenient way of shopping which has developed   57
recently is teleshopping. As well as the ability to order   115
goods chosen after viewing, users have access to a variety of   177
other services such as telephone directories and banking.   235
It is possible to use either a television or computer screen   295
and the goods listed are subsequently ordered by use of a   353
keypad or computer keyboard (or the telephone). After   307
ordering, the goods are delivered to the home and are   461
purchased by credit card debits.   493

Teleshopping is known as a 'retailing revolution' and helps
many people who are either housebound, too busy to go to the
shops, or who are very careful about choice of products.
These people have the choice of using videotex teleshopping
systems where text information on products is shown on a TV
or computer screen.   In order to use the system the television
equipment has to be linked to a central computer via the
telephone line.   An initial telephone call is made to connect
to the service and then, through this line, into teleshopping
schemes run by mail-order companies.   It is possible to view
the actual product on television, and to purchase the desired
one by credit card or, in a few cases, by means of a special
'electronic cheque' as it appears on the screen.   In France a
wider range of schemes is in existence and five million free
computer terminals for keying into the system have been
distributed to potential customers.

553
614
670
729
789
851
908
969
1031
1091
1152
1212
1272
1332
1387
1422

(284 words)

Exercise 74

An alternative to speaker presentations, as such, is
called "interactive multi-media". A computer is used to
store a variety of presentation material such as text,
pictures, sound and video clips. The person using the
computer presses a touch screen or cursor to activate
a specific part of the picture. This triggers an event,
eg the display, more text or the playing of a video clip.
The experience for the user is almost like playing a
video game but the intention is to educate and inform.
A recent example of multi-media is the "Virtual
Museum". This is a computerised library of visual
information so accessible that it allows the person using
it to walk round (to the sound of footsteps) in an
imaginary science or art museum. Upon 'entering' the
foyer he or she can click onto a particular choice of
subject material on display - choices include animation,
picture, static display of a work of art, treasure,
scientific marvel or discovery (recently updated) etc.

53
109
164
218
272
328
386
439
494
544
595
653
705
759
813
870
921
976

The person can then again walk through the various doorways and into the museum rooms. Having decided, one goes through the doorway, enters the chosen 'room' and views the moving computer graphic data, eg a video or animated clip about each topic, rotating each wall in turn to include the whole room. The main advantages of these interactive multi-media are that the person using the presentations can learn about what interests him or her at a chosen pace and from a vast choice of subjects.

1027
1085
1141
1196
1251
1308
1363
1420
1471

(294 words)

19

DIFFICULT SPELLINGS

Correct spelling, like punctuation, is essential to the production of good typewritten work, and you should never fail to consult a dictionary when there is uncertainty about the correct spelling of any word, and then seek to master it.

A selected list of difficult spellings is given below, and includes common words which often cause problems – such as *accommodate*, *gauge* and *seize* – as well as words which are in general business use. It is recommended that each page of the list should be typed, in order to impress the correct spelling on the mind. The meaning of the words is equally important, and a dictionary should be consulted where there is any doubt.

abhor	accommodation	adherence
abhorred	accumulate	adjournment
abolish	achieve	admissible
abscess	achieving	adolescent
accede	aching	advantageous
accept	acknowledge	advertise
access	acquiesce	advertisement
accessible	acquire	aerial
accommodate	adhere	affect

aggregate
aggrieved
aghast
agreeable
allege
allegiance
alliance
allotment
aluminium
amateur
ambiguity
ameliorate
amicable
ampersand
analogous
analyse
analysis
anomalous
appal
appalling
apparent
apparently
appealing
appendix
appropriate
argument
ascend
asset
assuage
asterisk
atrocious
auspicious
authentic
authenticity
auxiliary

bankruptcy
banquet
basically
bazaar
belief
believable

believe
beneficiaries
beneficiary
benefit
benefited
bias
bilateral
biography
bona fide
book-keeping
boycott
brilliance
brittle
budget
budgeting
buoy
bureaucracy
bureaucrat
by-election
by-law
by-product

cafeteria
calamitous
camouflage
canister
career
carousel
casualty
catalogue
catarrh
catastrophe
ceiling
changeable
chaos
chaotic
chargeable
chauffeur
chronological
coefficient
coincide
coinciding

collateral
colleague
colloquial
collusion
combustible
commitment
committal
compatibility
compatible
comprehensible
comprehensive
computerisation
compulsory
conceivable
conglomerate
connoisseur
conscientious
conspicuous
consummate
contentious
continent
controversy
conversation
conversion
corduroy
corollary
corroborate
corruptible
counterfeit
credible
crucial
cul-de-sac
curriculum

debacle
debar
debarred
debutante
decree
decreeing
defensible
defer

deferred
deficiency
deficient
demarcation
dependant (of)
dependent (on)
deprecate
depreciate
descendant
destructible
deterioration
deter
deterrent
develop
development
dial
dialling
diaphragm
diathermy
dilemma
disc
discern
discernible
discreet
discretion
discretionary
disk
dissatisfaction
disseminate
disservice
dissuade
doubtful
dubitable
dynamic

earnest
eavesdrop
ecclesiastical
ecstasy
edible
efficient
eligible

elucidate
embarrass
enamel
enamelled
encumbrance
encyclopaedia
entrepreneur
epitome
equanimity
equitable
equivalent
erstwhile
et cetera
etiquette
evaporate
exacerbate
exchange
exchangeable
excusable
excuse
exorbitant
extraneous
extra-curricular
extraditable
exuberant
eyewitness

facetious
facial
facile
fallacious
fatigue
feasible
February
fiasco
fibreglass
fictitious
flammable
flotation
focus
formally

formerly
  (previously)
fortuitous
freeing
fulfil
fulfilled
fulfilment

gauge
gauging
gazetteer
glossary
gratuitous
guarantor
gullible
gymnasium

haphazard
harass
hazardous
heterogeneous
honourable
honorary
humorist
humour
hydrangea
hygiene
hypothesis

idiosyncrasy
ignominious
illiteracy
illiterate
illusion
imminent
immovable
impracticable
impromptu
incognito
incur
incurred
independence

indict
indictment
infinitesimal
inflammable
ingenious
ingenuous
install
instalment
interim
irreducible
irresistible
itinerary

janitor
jargon
jeopardise
jewellery
judiciary
judicious
juxtaposition

kilogram
kilometre
kilowatt
kudos

label
labelled
laborious
liaison
libel
libellous
litigation

maestro
magnanimous
magnate
magnetise
maintenance
maisonette
malingerer
malleable

malpractice
manage
manageable
manoeuvre
marshalled
massacre
miniature
misapprehend
mis-statement
monetary
mortgage
mystery

naïve
necessary
necessitate
nomenclature
nondescript
nonplussed
notable
notice
noticeable
nowadays
nullify

obituary
obsession
occur
occurrence
omission
omit
omitted
onerous
ophthalmic
ostentatious
outrageous
overrate
oxy-acetylene

panel
panelled
paraffin

parallel
paralleled
parcel
parcelled
pastime
pecuniary
penultimate
perceivable
perceive
perceptible
peremptory
permissible
permit
persecute
personal
personnel
persuade
persuasive
pessimism
phantom
phenobarbitone
phenomenon
pharmaceutical
pharmacology
pharyngitis
phenomenal
phlox
phobia
phonetic
phosphorus
plagiarise
pneumatic
postcard
posthumous
practice (noun)
practise (verb)
precede
predecessor
prefer
preferred
principal (chief)
principle

proceed
process
proffer
programme (*but*
   computer
   program)
pronounce
pronounceable
pronunciation
propitious
pseudonym
psychology
purchasable
pursue
putrefy

quandary
quantitative
quarrel
quarrelled
queue

rateable
readdress
rearrange
receivable
reciprocate
recur
recurrence
removable
rendezvous
reprehensible
rescind
rescission
résumé
reversible
rhythm
rival
rivalled
rudimentary

sceptic
scepticism
scrutineer
secession
secretary
secretariat
segregate
seizable
seize
separate
silhouette
simultaneously
skiing
skilful
sophisticated
sovereignty
spontaneous
stationary (not
   moving)
stationery (en-
   velopes, etc)
statistician
stencilled
stereotyped
subsidiary
succeed
succession
succinct
sue
suggest
suggestible
suing
supercilious
supersede
surreptitious
susceptibility
susceptible
suspension
synonymous
synthesis

tautology
teetotaller
temporary
tinge
tingeing
trademark
transfer
transferable
transferred
triumph
tunnel
tunnelled

ubiquitous
unanimous
unilateral
unkempt
unnecessary
unparalleled
utilitarian

vapour
vaporise
vehicular
veil
vigorous
vigour
voracious

wilful
witticism
word processors

yardstick

zany
zapped
Zephyr
zoology

20

—— ABBREVIATIONS ——

Abbreviations are shortened forms of words and phrases – consisting in many cases only of initials – which have become established by common usage. The following list is not exhaustive, but includes most of the abbreviations in general business use and shows their meanings.

The use of the full stop will depend on whether open or closed punctuation is employed. Note, however, that certain signs and symbols should never take a full stop, for example the £ or $ sign, the ampersand (&) and @ (at). In addition, full stops should not be used after abbreviations of units of measurement, such as ft, mm and kg.

& and (ampersand)
@ at, for
A1 first class, first rate
a. a. r. against all risks
ab init. *ab initio* (Latin), from the beginning
abt about
a/c, acct account
 A/C account
accom. accommodation
ack acknowledge

AD *anno domini* (Latin), in the year of our Lord
ad., advt advertisement
ad lib. *ad libitum* (Latin), at pleasure
ad val. *ad valorem* (Latin), according to value
AGM Annual General Meeting
agt agreement; agent
a.m. *ante meridiem* (Latin), before noon

amt   amount
anon.   anonymous
ans.   answer
A/P   accounts payable
appro.   approval, approbation
approx.   approximate
appt(s)   appointments
A/R   accounts receivable
A/S   account sales
a.s.a.p.   as soon as possible
asst   assistant
av., ave   average

BA   Bachelor of Arts
bal.   balance
b/d   bring (brought) down
B/D   Bank Draft
B/E   bill of exchange
bel   believe
b/f   bring (brought) forward
bk   book
B/L   bill of lading
B/P   bill payable
B/R   bill receivable
Bro., Bros   brother, brothers
B/S   balance sheet; bill of sale
BSc   Bachelor of Science
bus   business
bx, bxs   box, boxes

c   cent(s)
C   centigrade, celsius
C/A   Capital Account
carr. pd   carriage paid
carr. fwd   carriage forward
cat.   catalogue
cc   cubic centimetre; carbon copy
c/d   carried down
cf.   compare
c/f   carried forward
C & F   cost and freight

ch., chap.   chapter
chq.   cheque
c.i.f.   cost, insurance and freight
cm   centimetre
C/N   credit note
co   company
Co.   Company
c/o   care of; carried over
COD   cash on delivery
col.   column
comm.   commission
cont.   continued
co-op   co-operative
cr.   credit, creditor
cres   crescent
CS   Civil Service
ctte   committee
cum div.   with the dividend
c.w.o.   cash with order

D/A   Deposit Account
DB   Day Book
D/D   Demand Draft
Deb.   Debenture
def   definitely
dely, d/y   delivery
dept   department
dev   develop
dft   draft
disc.   discount
div.   dividends; division
D/N   Debit Note
do.   ditto (the same)
doz.   dozen
D/P   documents against payment
dr.   debtor, debit
Dr   Doctor or Dear
d/s   days after sight
D.V.   *Deo volente* (Latin), God Willing

ea.   each
ed.   edition, editor
e.g.   for example (*exempli gratia*)
enc.   enclosure(s)
entd   entered
E&OE   errors and omissions excepted
EPT   Excess Profit Tax
esp.   especially
Esq.   Esquire
est.   established; estimated
et al.   *et alia* (Latin), and others
ETA   estimated time of arrival
etc.   *et cetera* (Latin), and the rest
ETD   estimated time of departure
et seq.   *et sequentia* (Latin), and the following
ex.   without or exercise
exch.   exchange
ex div., x. div.   without dividends
ex int.   not including interest
exors   executors
exp.   express or experience
exs   expenses

f, fr.   franc(s)
F, Fahr.   Fahrenheit
f.a.a.   free of all average (used in marine insurance)
FAO   for the attention of
f.a.q.   free alongside quay; fair average quality
f.a.s.   free alongside ship
Feb   February
fcp, fcap   foolscap
f.d.   free docks
ffly   faithfully
f.i.f.o.   first in, first out

fig[s]   figure(s)
f.t.i.   free of income tax
fo, fol.   folio
FO   Firm Order
f.o.b.   free on board
f.o.r.   free on rail
fp.   fully paid
fr.   from
Fri   Friday
frt   freight
ft   foot, feet
fwd   forward

g   gram(me)
GA   general average (insurance)
gen.   general
GM   General Manager
GMT   Greenwich Mean Time
gntee(s)   guarantee(s)
Gov.   Governor
Govt.   Government
gr.   grain, grammar
gr. wt.   gross weight

HMSO   Her Majesty's Stationery Office
HO   Head Office
Hon.   Honorary, Honourable
h.p.   horse power
HP   hire purchase
HQ   headquarters
hr, hrs   hour(s)

ib, ibid.   *ib idem* (Latin), in the same place
IB   Invoice Book
IBI   Invoice Book Inwards
i/c   in charge
i.e.   *id est* (Latin), that is
I/F   insufficient funds (banking)
immed   immediate

IMF International Monetary Fund
Inc. incorporated
incon inconvenient/ce
ins. insurance
inst. instant, current month
int. interest
inv. invoice
IOU I owe you
ital. italics
IQ Intelligence Quotient

J/A Joint Account
Jan January
JP Justice of the Peace
Jun., Jr Junior

kg, kilo kilogram(me)
kl kilolitre(s)
km kilometre(s)
kw kilowatts

£ pound sterling
l, lit. litre(s)
lat. latitude
lb pound (weight)
l.c. lower case
L/C Letter of Credit
Led. Ledger
LGA Local Government Authority; Local Government Area
l.i.f.o. last in, first out
long. longitude
Ltd limited

m metre(s), minutes, million
max. maximum
MC Master of Ceremonies
m/d months after date
med. medium
mem., memo. memorandum

Messrs *Messieurs* (French), Gentlemen
mfg manufacturing
mfr manufacturer
mg milligram
mgr manager
min. minimum, minute
MIP Marine Insurance Policy
misc miscellaneous
ml millilitre(s)
mm millimetre(s)
Mme Madame
MO Medical Officer; money order
Mon Monday
MP Member of Parliament; Military Police
m.p.h. miles per hour
m/s months after sight; metre per second
ms(s). manuscript(s)
MSc Master of Science

n.a. not available
N/A no advice; not acceptable (banking); not applicable
NB *nota bene* (Latin), mark well, note well
necy necessary
nem. con. *nemine contradicente* (Latin), no one contradicting
N/F no funds (banking)
nil *nihil* (Latin), nothing
N/m no mark
N/O no orders (trading)
nom. nominal
NP Notary Public
NPV no par value
nr near

% per cent

%0   per thousand
o/a   on account of
o/c   over charge; officer commanding; out of charge
o/d   on demand
O/D   overdraft, overdrawn
OK   all correct
O&M   Organisation and Methods
o/p   out of print
op. cit.   *opere citato* (Latin), in the work cited
opp.   opposed, opposite or opportunities
OR   owner's risk
ord.   ordinary
o/s   out of stock; outstanding

p., pp.   page, pages
p.a.   *per annum* (Latin), yearly
PAYE   pay as you earn (taxation)
p.c.   per cent; post card
PC   Police constable
p/c   price current
p.c.b.   petty cash book
pcl   parcel
pcs   pieces
pd   paid
per   by
per capita   by the head
per prop, pp   *per procurationem* (Latin), on behalf of
pkg.   package
P & L   Profit and Loss
Plc   Public Limited Company
p.m.   *post meridiem* (Latin), afternoon or evening
p.n   promissory note
P.O.   postal order; post office
pp.   parcel post
p. & p.   postage and packing

pr, pr.   pair, price
pref.   preference, preferred
prepd   prepared
prima facie   at first sight
Prof.   Professor
pro forma   as a matter of form
pro tem.   *pro tempore* (Latin), for the time being
PS   postscript
PTO   please turn over
PV   per value

qu.   query, question
quan.   quantity
qr   quarter

R/D   refer to drawer (banking)
re.   with reference to, concerning
rec   receive
rec(t)   receipt
recd   received
recom   recommend
ref.   reference
refd   referred
reg., regd   registered
rep.   report; representative
req   required
resp   responsible
retd   returned
rd   road
rly   railway
rm   ream
R/p   reply paid
RSVP   *Repondez, s'il vous plait* (French), please reply

$ dollar (money)
Sat   Saturday
SB   sales book
sch.   school; schedule
sec.   second or secretary

sep separate
sgn sign(ed)
sh shall
shd should
sig(s) signature
S/N shipping note
soc. society
spec. specification, speculation
sq. square
SS steamship
St. Saint; street; station
std standard
STD Subscriber Trunk Dialling
stet let it stand
stg sterling (money)
stk stock
suff sufficient
Sun Sunday

temp temporary
thro through
Thurs Thursday
TMO telegraph money order
TO, t/o turnover
Tr. Trustee
TT telegraphic transfer
Tue Tuesday

u.c. upper case
ult. *ultimo* (Latin), last month; ultimatum

u/w underwriter

v., vs versus; against
var. variety
VAT Value-added tax
VHF very high frequency
via by way of, through
viz. *videlicet* (Latin), namely
vol. volume

w with
W/B Waybill
wd would
Wed Wednesday
w.e.f. with effect from
wh which
whf wharf
wi will
wk(s) week; weeks
w.p.m. words per minute
wt, wgt weight

x.d. ex dividend (without dividend)
x.int. ex interest (without interest)

yr(s) year(s)
yrs yours

KEYS TO THE EXERCISES

Key to Exercise 41

Nowadays it is possible to present information in an exciting and interesting way when giving a lecture or audio-visual presentation to an audience. The operator can use video projectors connected directly to a computer, and from there to a television screen. It can also be linked to conventional overhead projectors to show the image on screen and such methods can also be used in colleges and schools. The viewers can then see exactly what is stored on the computer being transferred to a large television screen.

Other exciting innovations are the availability of computers which are portable and work from batteries. They allow the facilities of the electronic office to be carried in a small and lightweight machine which can be used on cars, trains and aircraft whilst travelling worldwide. Afterwards, the user returns to his permanent office location and links into the computer network to integrate his new material to the system.

Key to Exercise 42

HOME ADDRESS

Today's Date

Westoby & Sheerwater PLC
369 Church St Gardens
EDMONTON
N9 7YT

Dear Sirs

POST AS PERSONAL ADMINISTRATOR - PERSONNEL DEPT

I am enclosing my application form for the above post
in your Company.

Should I be fortunate enough to be considered as a
possible candidate I would be able to attend an
interview at any time to suit you except on Monday,
14 July, when I have to attend a Conference in
Glasgow on behalf of my Company.

Yours faithfully

A L Jones (Mr)

enc

Key to Exercise 43

WESTOBY & SHEERWATER PLC
369 Church Street Gardens
EDMONTON   N9 7YT

JOB   APPLICATION   FORM

Title of Job .... Dept ....

APPLICANT'S FULL NAME (BLOCK CAPITALS)

SURNAME .... FIRST NAMES ....

ADDRESS ....

.... POST CODE ....

DATE OF BIRTH .... NATIONALITY ....

EDUCATIONAL QUALIFICATIONS (Please give dates)

School ....

....

College ....

Other ....

Typing Speed (if applicable) .... wpm

EXPERIENCE (Please give dates)

Job Title   Company Name

....

....

....

Salary Required ...... pa

REASONS FOR APPLYING FOR THIS POST

....

....

Signed .... Date ....

Jonathan Henry Miller & Sons PLC

ESTATE AGENTS
9 WEST FRONT
CAMBRIDGE CB1 8DR
Tel 0223 686 00777   *FAX 0223 8634435*

Our ref DM/JR/BEECH

19 March 19--

Mr F R Finlay
Drover's Cottage
High Street
HORRINGER
IP32 1QR

Dear Mr Finlay

RE PURCHASE OF FLAT AT 15 BEECH MEWS E9 0XLL

I am writing to confirm that I have put forward your
offer of £95,500 to Miss Baine, the Vendor. She has
accepted this offer with the proviso that, as the
figure is lower than the asking price of £105,000,
she is not prepared to include the carpets, curtains
and light fittings in the sale.

Please let me know as soon as possible what your
views are.

Yours sincerely

DOROTHY MILLER
Manager

Key to Exercise 46

HOME ADDRESS

Date

The Manager
Westbury Commercial Bank PLC
The Maltings
KING'S ACRE   Suffolk
IP25 6LD

Dear Sir

I am writing to enquire whether your bank would be
prepared to make loan or overdraft facilities of
£2,000 available to me.

Next month I am commencing trading as a Financial
Services Consultant and I urgently need to purchase a
new electronic typewriter for £200 and a word
processor for £800. Additionally I shall need other
small items of office equipment. Therefore, a
business loan or overdraft would be essential.

I have had current, Higher Rate Deposit and Tessa
accounts with your bank for several years now and,
should you find it necessary, I would be prepared to
provide appropriate security such as life
insurance policies.

Thank you for your help in this matter. I should
appreciate a reply as soon as possible as the
equipment is urgently required.

Yours faithfully

NAME IN CAPS

Jonathan Henry Miller & Sons PLC

ESTATE AGENTS
9 WEST FRONT
CAMBRIDGE CB1 8DR
Tel 0223 686 00777   *FAX 0223 8634435*

Our ref   SJ/BC

3 June 199–

Dr Frederic Avey
10 Birch Avenue
Church Street
EDMONTON   N9 9XV

Dear Dr Avey

SALE OF THE THATCHED COTTAGE, LYLE LANE, GODMANSTON,
CAMBRIDGE CB19 1BR

We are pleased .to advise you that we have placed an
advertisement in a local paper with a large
distribution area offering your property for sale at
the agreed price of £150,000. The paper will be
published on Friday of this week and we anticipate a
good response to our advertising.

If we receive any offers for your property, we shall
immediately contact you and take instructions
regarding the sale. It is always advisable to be
prepared to accept an offer if this falls within your
financial expectation, and we have priced your
property at a suitable figure to enable you to
do this.

If we can be of any further assistance, please do not
hesitate to contact us. In the meantime we will
continue to show prospective purchasers round
your property.

Yours sincerely

Sandra Johnson
Property Consultant

Key to Exercise 49

MEMORANDUM

TO   Sandra Johnson, Property Consultant

FROM   Natalie Miller, Executive Director

DATE   4 April 199-

ADVERTISEMENTS FOR NEW PROPERTIES

I am sending you the 3 latest advertisements which we need to publish in the "Huntingdon and Cambridge Weekly Herald" this week.

Please check that all the details are correct - price, description, etc and then notify the clients that we are advertising their properties for sale as from next Friday's edition.

The photographs are arriving from the processors tomorrow. I think you will find that the "Herald" needs to have our advertisements 4 days before publication. This is a new expanding local paper with a distribution which covers a wide area around Cambridge and Huntingdon and we should have some good response to our advertisement.

I would appreciate any comments on potential improvements etc which you may wish to make as I sometimes feel that our descriptions of properties could be more dynamic and appealing.

1)   Deceptively spacious thatched cottage with good sized grounds, situated in quiet village opposite church - 3 beds, 2 rec, garage, stable block and barn. £150,000. Ref QD 46. (GODMASTON)

2)   Beautifully refurbished detached house in semi-rural position with large gardens, garage, 3 beds, large kitchen. £132,000. Ref QD 47. (CLAYTONBURY)

3)   Just reduced for quick sale - 4 bed terraced Georgian house in city centre, 3 reception rooms, off-street parking for 3 cars, short distance from river (mooring rights also available) £140,000. Ref QD 48. (CAMBRIDGE)

Please let me know as soon as you have organised this and send me a copy of the PROOFS.

Key to Exercise 50

T H E   P R O P E R T Y   L E T T I N G   C E N T R E

Head Office   24 Lynton Close   Elm End Road.
WATFORD   WD3 7KKM

Telephone 0923 1200099   FAX 0923 1226565

Our ref: BKC/WM/ht

4 September 199-

Mr D A V Jackson
Avenida de Alvarode
Vascenceles 2993
2711 SINTRA
Portugal

Dear Mr Jackson

Re: 15 Beechwood Mews, Harewood St, Potters Bar

Further to our visit to the above flat on
31 August 199-, we are pleased to confirm that, as
agreed, we have placed details of the property on our
books at a rental charge of £520 per calendar month.

As you are aware, the rental income will be inclusive
of maintenance, ground rent, and water rate for which
you are currently responsible. The services such as
Gas, Telephone and Electricity will be payable by
the Tenants who will be informed by us to sign for
the source of supply prior to occupation.

We always advertise our properties only to
professional persons and we take up their references
on your behalf. A deposit of one month's rental plus
£100 booking fee is paid to us plus the one month's
rental in advance. We then deduct our fees from this
sum and forward to you an account plus the balance
of the monies due to you. If you require any
alteration to this arrangement, ie for this Company
to pay the monies into an English bank account on
your behalf we shall be pleased to do this for you.

2
4 September 199–
Mr D A V Jackson

It may be that you will find you will need to make
use of our full property management service whilst
you are staying for an indefinite period abroad, and,
if you require any further information, please do not
hesitate to contact us. In the meantime I enclose
our brochure containing details of the full
management service we provide.

Yours sincerely

WENDY MACPHERSON
Property Letting Manager

enc

Key to Exercise 51

THE PROPERTY LETTING CENTRE

THIS BROCHURE is to give you information regarding
our two services of property letting. Both services
include a free valuation of your property by our
expert valuer to ascertain that a correct rental is
to be charged.

The first, which is a full management service,
guarantees that this Company will find you a suitable
professional person to rent your property for six
monthly (or one yearly) periods. The Company takes
up full financial and personal references on your
behalf and collects the rents as and when these
become due. A full Tenancy Agreement is drawn up and
signed by both parties. The full management service
means that you have peace of mind as, should any
repairs etc become necessary, the Company arranges
for the appropriate work to be carried out, and debits
your account accordingly. This is a particularly
suitable service for owners who are too busy to
supervise the lettings personally or who are living
abroad. There is a charge of 12 per cent for this
service.

We offer the second service which is a PART
MANAGEMENT SERVICE where this Company guarantees to
find a suitable professional person to rent your
property for six monthly or one yearly periods. The
Company takes up full financial and personal.
references on your behalf and collects the rents as
and when due. A Full Tenancy Agreement is drawn up
and signed by both parties. This is a suitable
service for owners who are able to personally
supervise the letting and arrange their own repairs.
There is a charge of 10 per cent for this service.
Should you require to change over from the part
management service to full management at any time
during the tenancy period this can be arranged at a
fee of two per cent extra.

In both services the Tenant will be asked to provide
a deposit of ONE MONTH'S RENTAL in advance and to pay
his or her rent by standing order at a bank or
through a building society.

Key to Exercise 52

```
                      35 East Barnes Avenue
                            Dykes Burn
                          MIDDLESBROUGH
                            Cleveland
                            NT3 37LK

              Telephone No 0642 87 224439

24 September 199-

The Manager
Property Letting Centre
24 Lynton Close
Elm End Road
WATFORD      WD3 7KM

Dear Sir

With reference to your advertisement in today's
edition of the 'Daily Provincial and Cleveland Echo',
I shall be grateful if you will kindly send me as
soon as possible details of the two flats you have
available - reference numbers G789 and G901.

I am commencing work in Central London on 10 October
and am urgently in need of a fully furnished two
bedroom flat near to a railway station that would be
convenient for commuting to Liverpool Street station.
The maximum rental I am prepared to pay is £130 per
week or £550 per calendar month.

The flat must have an automatic washing machine,
tumble dryer, fridge, freezer, cooker extractor hood,
and some form of central heating.  I do also need
good parking facilities to be available nearby,
preferably on the premises.

In order to save time I am enclosing the names and
addresses of two referees to whom you can write and
you will note that one is my employer in
Middlesbrough for whom I have worked for five years.
```

2
24 September 199-
Property Letting Centre

I plan to visit London on 28 September and, if I like
the flat after viewing it, I shall be prepared to
sign a contract immediately and move in on 30
September or as soon after that date as is possible.

Thank you for your help in this matter.

Yours faithfully

Belinda Richardson (Miss)

enc

Key to Exercise 53

——— ABC TRAVEL LODGE ———
CLUBS PLC

PRINCETON HOUSE
23–30 TWINING ROAD LONDON SW2V 1QT

Telephone 041 3456 4537566   Fax 041 3456 467388

Our ref blj/rh/2349866/2/3
14 September 199-

Miss B L Cross
22 Little Heath Close
Muswell Hill
LONDON   N10 8UK

Dear Miss Cross

re HOLIDAY BOOKING NO 2349866/2/3

Thank you for your letter of 10 September regarding
yours and Mrs Mortimer's accommodation for the above
holiday. I am pleased to confirm that we have
arranged your booking as follows:

Luxury apartment with balcony, 2 en suite bathrooms,
2 bedrooms, use of Health Club, sauna, swimming pool,
jacuzzi (25 October to 10 November inclusive).

The address of your hotel is: WAVECREST HOTEL, DEL
MAR, SAN DIEGO, CALIFORNIA, USA, and I confirm that a
Holiday Club rental car (Granada) has been booked
and will be awaiting you at San Diego airport on
24 October when you land at 5.30 pm.

Air tickets and all travel documents with Blue Sky
Airways will be sent to you 10 days before departure,
together with the vouchers for the six weeks'
vacation in Del Mar.

You will also receive confirmation of your free one
week car hire and we do suggest that, should you wish
to add additional weeks to the car hire, you book it
with us as we now have a very favourable car hire
rate available as a special offer.

2
14 September 199-
Miss B L Cross

Thank you for using our travel services, and please
do not hesitate to contact us should you have any
further queries.

May we wish you both a very enjoyable holiday.

Yours sincerely

Director of ABC Travel

Key to Exercise 57

LIST OF SUBJECTS

Accountancy	Dietetics	Mathematics	Printing
Advertising	Economics	Metallurgy	Refrigeration
Aeronautics	Elocution	Mineralogy	Salesmanship
Architecture	Engineering	Mining	Shipping
Arithmetic	English	Music	Shorthand
Banking	First-Aid	Needlework	Sociology
Book-keeping	Geography	Optics	Telecommunications
Building	History	Pharmacy	Television
Calculations	Insurance	Photography	Theatre
Chemistry	Investment	Physics	Transport
Commerce	Journalism	Poetry	Typewriting

Key to Exercise 58

THE GRAND NATIONAL

Year	Horse	Jockey	Owner
1972	Well to Do	G Thorner	Capt T Forster
1973	Red Rum	B Fletcher	Mr N Le Mare
1974	Red Rum	B Fletcher	Mr N Le Mare
1975	L'Escargot	T Carberry	Mr R Guest
1976	Rag Trade	J Burke	Mr P Raymond
1977	Red Rum	T Stack	Mr N Le Mare
1978	Lucius	B R Davis	Mrs D Whitaker
1979	Rubstic	M Barnes	Mr J Douglas
1980	Ben Nevis	C Fenwick	Mr R Stewart Jun
1981	Aldaniti	R Champion	Mrs V Embericos

Key to Exercise 59

ARABIC AND ROMAN NUMERALS

Arabic	Roman small	Roman capitals	Arabic	Roman small	Roman capitals
1	i	I	15	xv	XV
2	ii	II	16	xvi	XVI
3	iii	III	17	xvii	XVII
4	iv	IV	18	xviii	XVIII
5	v	V	19	xix	XIX
6	vi	VI	20	xx	XX
7	vii	VII	30	xxx	XXX
8	viii	VIII	40	xl	XL
9	ix	IX	50	l	L
10	x	X	60	lx	LX
11	xi	XI	70	lxx	LXX
12	xii	XII	80	lxxx	LXXX
13	xiii	XIII	90	xc	XC
14	xiv	XIV	100	c	C

Key to Exercise 60

THE PRINCIPAL NATIONAL DAILIES

Paper	Proprietors	Circulation in 19-- (millions)
Daily Express	Trafalgar House	2.4
Daily Mail	Associated Newspapers	1.9
Daily Mirror	Reed Publishing Holdings	3.6
Daily Star	Trafalgar House	0.9
Daily Telegraph	Daily Telegraph	1.3
Financial Times	Pearson Longman	0.2
Guardian	Guardian and Manchester Evening News	0.4
Morning Star	Morning Star Co-op Society	0.03
Sun	News International	3.8
The Times	News International	0.3

Key to Exercise 61

ELECTRA MACHINE

Quarterly Sales

Branch	March	June	Sept	Dec
Southampton	136	210	195	187
Portsmouth	125	167	154	170
Liverpool	103	141	139	126
Birmingham	214	230	179	223
Manchester	212	176	194	182
Leeds	317	265	276	284
Sheffield	284	314	237	330
Burnley	147	201	169	229
Middlesbrough	231	198	217	186
Cardiff	246	312	256	306
Swansea	193	224	184	219
Newport	231	189	209	196
Totals	2,439	2,627	2,409	2,638

INDEX

7214